HUME PAPERS ON PUBLIC POLICY
Volume 8, No. 3

THE SETTLEMENT OF LEGAL DISPUTES. AN ASSESSMENT OF RECENT REFORM MEASURES

THE DAVID HUME INSTITUTE

HUME PAPERS ON PUBLIC POLICY
Volume 8 No. 3

THE SETTLEMENT OF LEGAL DISPUTES. AN ASSESSMENT OF RECENT REFORM MEASURES

EDINBURGH UNIVERSITY PRESS

© David Hume Institute 2001

Edinburgh University Press
22 George Square, Edinburgh.

Typeset in Times New Roman by
WestKey Limited, Falmouth, Cornwall
and printed and bound in Great Britain by
Page Bros Ltd, Norwich Norfolk

A CIP record of this book is available from the British Library

ISBN 0 7486 1548 2

Contents

Foreword	vii
1. Conditional Fees *Stella Yarrow*	1
2. Disclosure, Experts and Information in Litigation *Paul Fenn, Alastair Gray and Neil Rickman*	11
3. Reform of Legal Aid in Scotland *Frank H Stephen*	23
4. Cost Shifting and Pre-trial Settlement *Brian G M Main and Andrew Park*	42

Contributors

Paul Fenn is Norwich Union Professor of Insurance Studies at the Nottingham Business School.

Alastair Gray is Reader in Health Economics and Director of the Health Economics Research Centre at the University of Oxford.

Brian G M Main is Professor of Economics at the University of Edinburgh and Director of The David Hume Institute.

Andrew Park is Lecturer in Economics at the University of Strathclyde.

Neil Rickman is Reader in Economics at the University of Surrey and Research Affiliate with the Centre for Economic Policy Research.

Frank H Stephen is Professor of Economics at the University of Strathclyde and Adviser to the Justice and Home Affairs Committee of the Scottish Parliament.

Stella Yarrow is Quintin Hogg Research Fellow in Law at the University of Westminster.

Foreword

This volume brings together a set of papers that formed the basis of a conference held by the Institute to examine the important matter of resolving disputes through the courts. It has long been recognised that the activity of the courts in allowing disputing parties to come to a settlement is of vital importance in many aspects of economic life, not least among which is the matter of commercial contracts. It is also recognised that even those disputes which go nowhere near the law courts are heavily influenced by what the parties know and expect will occur should their dispute ever reach the courts. This last phenomenon is known as negotiating in the shadow of the law. It is, therefore, a matter of no small importance to the economic efficiency of society that the law courts effect their dispute resolution activity in as efficient a manner as possible. To this end, the procedural and other rules that condition the activity of the courts are continuously the subject of scrutiny and, at times, of policy innovation. The last decade or so has been marked by a relatively high level of activity in this field and the conference, held by the Institute on 30 May 2000 and entitled *Settlement of Legal Disputes: An Assessment of Recent Reform Measures*, sought to examine certain aspects of recent innovations.

A widely discussed innovation, namely the move to conditional fees, was the subject of a presentation by Stella Yarrow. Under this arrangement (now common in England and Wales and making increasing inroads in Scotland) the legal agent (solicitor) receives no fee if the case is lost but is entitled to an uplift on the fee if the case is won. This is not the same as the American practice of contingent fees where the lawyer's fee is calculated as part of the quantum of damages (if any) secured, thereby rendering the lawyer an interested party in the case. Yarrow discussed the findings from four distinct studies she has conducted on this topic. The new arrangements seem to be working well. Solicitors tend to be rather pessimistic in estimating the chances of success of a case and some consumers do not fully comprehend how the success fee operates (this will, in any case, soon be recoverable from the losing party), but by and large there has been a successful shift to this system of meeting legal costs. Not only does this have the immediate effect of relieving civil legal aid of involvement but it also extends the scope of cases that can be brought into the legal system, thereby addressing what is widely perceived to be 'unmet need'.

Neil Rickman presented some empirical results of a study on the workings of rules of legal discovery that he conducted along with fellow researchers, Paul Fenn and Alistair Gray. This study relied on the experience of a sample of medical malpractice cases as they moved through the legal system to disposition or settlement. Legal cases often begin with both parties having views (based on private information) about their prospects. To the extent that their information (and interpretations of it) differ, it may prove difficult/costly to resolve the dispute. One can think of the litigation process as providing a continual opportunity for parties to transfer information to each other, thereby supposedly aiding settlement prospects. Such opportunities can be formal (such as those provided by disclosure of documents) of informal (such as those provided by responses to settlement offers). With policy interest in recent years focusing on reducing the costs and delay of litigation, it is clear that this is an important area of research.

Rickman's presentation examined the use of disclosure and expert evidence in a sample of negligence cases (largely medical ones) brought against NHS Trusts between 1978 and 1998. Disclosure typically took place within 6 months of a writ being served whereas the expert reports appeared, on average, after almost two years. An important question is the effects of these events on the likelihood of settlement, so the research analysed this for a subsample of cases closed between 1990 and 1995. The results suggest that expert reports increased the subsequent probability of settlement, while disclosure reduced it. This distinction is new and interesting; it is consistent with the conjecture that different types of information are being transferred by these different events. The paper suggests that disclosure may reduce settlement chances because it involves the handing over of material that makes the other side stronger, while experts (on average) improve settlement chances because they resolve uncertainty that both sides face (e.g. on prognosis). If confirmed by further work, this would have interesting policy implications. For example, Lord Woolf's proposal that medical negligence cases should typically rely on one expert (shared by the parties) would be consistent with this interpretation of expert evidence.

Frank Stephen presented an analysis of Criminal Legal Aid data for Scotland in which he examined the impact of a move to fixed fees for aspects of summary criminal cases. To demonstrate the attraction of such a move, he showed a graph of the time series of criminal legal aid expenditure in Scotland over the period 1980–1997. The sharply rising trend was unmistakable and a marked jump was also evident post 1992, a period when the housing market was in recession. This raises the prospect of possible supplier-induced demand whereby cases are being 'padded' to create work. But Stephen favours an alternative explanation that rests on the increased volume of criminal cases in the system increasing delay and, hence, legal costs. He also points to a marked inefficiency in the system whereby individuals who plead not guilty only to change their plea to one of guilty on appearance in court secure the benefit of legally-aided advice and scrutiny of the prosecution case. But those who plead guilty at the outset have no recourse to legal aid in coming to their decision or in plea bargaining. This creates an unnecessary and artificial incentive to plead not guilty. Finally Stephen examined the likely impact of the introduction of fixed fees to the criminal legal aid system. This he predicted will make relatively little difference to the overall legal aid bill but it may sharply alter the distribution of legal aid earnings towards the larger partnerships and away from the smaller groups.

Using a rather unusual methodology for this area, Brian Main and Andy Park reported the results of several sets of experiments in the course of which individuals were observed in controlled laboratory conditions negotiating under various 'cost-shifting' rules. The best known variation in such arrangements is the difference between the UK (loser pays) and the USA (each side pays its own legal fees irrespective of outcome). But other variations exist within the UK, for example where the defendant who has made what in retrospect (in the light of the judge's decision) is seen as a generous pre-trial settlement offer is exempt from part of the costs that they would otherwise have to bear. The High Court in England and Wales has extended a version of this arrangement to claimants, and the Court of Session in Scotland made a short-lived innovation along the same lines in 1996. The evidence from the experiments conducted by Main and Park reveals that such rules have remarkably little impact on the propensity of the parties to settle out of court, but do influence the level of settlement that is likely to be reached in any out of court agreement. This evidence suggests that at least part of the policy-makers' motivation in this field is misplaced.

The David Hume Institute is delighted to be able to bring together this collection of conference papers which relate to what is an essential, but often overlooked, aspect of commercial life. As always, it is necessary to clarify that the Institute itself holds no collective view on these policy matters. We do, however, feel that we can recommend this work as a useful contribution to our understanding of this important area where a discussion of current policy is extremely timely.

Brian G M Main
Director
The David Hume Institute

Conditional Fees

Stella Yarrow

Conditional fee agreements (CFAs) were introduced into England and Wales as a new method of paying lawyers. Under CFAs, the lawyer is paid only if successful. This paper evaluates their impact, drawing on a programme of research into CFAs carried out between 1996–2000. The research consisted of two main elements: a survey of solicitors who provided details of a sample of CFA cases, and qualitative interviews with solicitors, barristers and clients.[1] The studies focused on personal injury, as this is the area of law in which CFAs have become best established.

How CFAs operate in England and Wales

Conditional fees were part of the programme of the Conservative government instituted in the late 1980s to reform the legal profession by increasing competition and removing restrictive practices. Agreements where the lawyer's fees depended on the outcome of the case were previously legally unenforceable in contentious business in England and Wales. Such fee arrangements were also prohibited by the ethical codes of both branches of legal profession in England and Wales. The profession regarded them as posing an unacceptable conflict of interest to the lawyer. The Government rejected the option of permitting lawyers to take a percentage of the damages, as in the USA. Instead, it adopted the Scottish model of speculative actions, where the lawyer received their normal fees only when successful. It added a provision that the lawyer could charge an extra percentage of those fees to reflect the risk of not being paid at all. (In fact, in England and Wales, speculative fees were also a common, albeit unofficial practice, in personal injury actions).

---

[1] This article draws on four studies: i) a survey of 200 CFA cases (Yarrow, 1997), funded by the Lord Chancellor's Advisory Committee on Legal Education and Conduct ii) a follow-up study of the sample of cases, funded by the Nuffield Foundation, iii) a study of clients in conditional fee cases, funded by the Nuffield Foundation (Yarrow and Abrams, 1999) iv) a study of the Bar and conditional fees (Abrams and Yarrow, forthcoming). The author acknowledges the help of her co-researcher Pamela Abrams, with whom this article was discussed.

CFAs were initially permitted in three areas of law, personal injury, insolvency and cases to the European Court of Human Rights. In successful cases, the losing side pays the lawyer's basic costs but the lawyer can also charge the client an additional success fee of up to 100% of those costs. In personal injury cases, the Law Society recommended a voluntary cap of 25% on the percentage of damages that the solicitor could take. CFAs are generally used by claimants in an action. They can insure themselves against the risk of having to pay the other side's costs if they lose, by buying an 'after-the-event' insurance policy. This risk could be a major deterrent to using CFAs. Initially, the market was dominated by one insurance scheme, Accident Line Protect, which was backed by the Law Society.

The Labour party, once in power, adopted enthusiastically the previous Government's policy of promoting CFAs. In 1997, the Government announced that it would extend CFAs to most other kinds of civil case. A principal argument used by both the previous and current governments in favour of CFAs was that they extend access to justice by enabling people who were not eligible for legal aid but could not afford to pay a lawyer to obtain legal advice. Another policy aim for both governments was to increase competition by removing a restrictive practice. An added advantage, according to the current administration, was that CFAs would prevent weaker cases from clogging up the legal system, because they will not attract commercial funding. In fact, though, very few personal injury cases get as far as the courts.

Government promotion of CFAs should also be seen in the context of rising spending on civil legal aid. If CFAs proved a viable method of funding cases, they would be a means of putting the onus on lawyers to finance litigation instead of the State. The Conservative government denied that CFAs would be used as a substitute for legal aid; instead it was an additional funding method (Hansard, 15 May 1995). However, it also suggested that legal aid might no longer be provided in cases where CFAs were available (Lord Chancellor's Department, 1995; Lord Chancellor's Department, 1996). The current government took this policy further. It pointed out that in the six years to 1997, the cost of civil and family legal aid tripled to £671 million. At the same time, the number of cases supported fell (Lord Chancellor's Department, 1997). CFAs were one means of addressing this problem.

The Government's original intention, announced in 1997, was to remove legal aid from most money claims, on the basis that CFAs would fund them instead. This would enable public funding to be targeted to what it regards as social welfare priorities. An alliance of the Law Society, Bar Council, the advice sector, and consumer and voluntary organisations campaigned against this proposal. It had only limited success. The government made some concessions, for example, postponing the abolition of legal aid for clinical negligence. However, the withdrawal of funding from most personal injury cases and some other categories of case went ahead on 1 April, 2000.

In Scotland, by comparison, the Home Affairs Minister, Henry McLeish, was unenthusiastic about switching from legal aid to CFAs. He pointed out that 80% of legal aid spending on reparation actions is recovered (Scottish Office, 1998). And while the Legal Aid Board in England and Wales did not oppose Government policy, the Scottish Legal Aid Board took the view that, as cases for which CFAs are suitable were self-financing, the move was neither necessary not desirable (SLAB, 1998). One reason for the difference may be that civil legal aid accounts for only one-third of the legal aid bill in Scotland, but two-thirds in England.

The impact on clients

As noted above, one of the policy aims of CFAs was to open up competition in the legal profession by removing a restriction on how lawyers operated. The previous Government painted a picture of how consumers would shop around for lower success fees and lawyers rival each other by price-cutting. It relied on market mechanisms to regulate success fees. Claiming that over-regulation would limit the cases that solicitors would take on, it rejected proposals to put a statutory cap on the percentage of damages that clients could lose. Instead, the agreement between lawyer and client only had to say if there was such a limit, and, if so, what it was. It set the success fee at 100% of basic costs (ten times the original suggestion of 10%). The only other statutory mechanism to regulate success fees was the client's right to ask the courts to review them.

It is well known, however, that markets in professional services often operate poorly because of principal-agent problems. There is a conflict of interest between the two parties and an asymmetry of information between them. It is difficult for the client to monitor either the lawyer's input of effort or the quality of the outcome, including whether the solicitor has made a correct judgement as to when it is the client's best interest to cease pursuing the claim (Bowles, 1996). While these problems arise in any lawyer-client relationship, they are particularly acute when the lawyer is paid with a CFA for the following reasons.

The method of calculating the success fee poses two major difficulties for clients. The basic principle is that the success fee is an additional percentage of the solicitor's basic costs; the percentage is calculated by dividing the prospects of failure by the prospects of success. The success fee should be proportionate to the chances of success in the individual's case. The higher the risk of losing, the higher the success fee that would be justifiable. Clients are, however, dependent on the solicitor's view of the case's prospects of success. A client could not easily challenge the statement by a solicitor that, for example, the maximum success fee of 100% is appropriate in their case. The basic costs themselves are calculated with reference to the number of hours spent by the lawyer on the case. This poses the usual problem when lawyers are paid on an hourly basis: how the client can ensure that the lawyer spends the optimum number of hours on the case.

The very complexity of the fee arrangements makes the usual information asymmetry particularly marked. This put CFA clients, who are generally relatively inexperienced consumers of legal services, at a considerable disadvantage. Clients in personal injury cases are also often particularly vulnerable because they are suffering the effects of an accident, particularly at the early stage of appointing a solicitor and agreeing fee arrangements.

Research on success fees provided some evidence that clients were unable to ensure that their interests were protected. A survey of CFA cases showed that solicitors, when calculating the success fee to be written into the contract with the client, did not consistently relate them to the chances of success. There was also a large proportion of cases which solicitors estimated had a relatively high risk of failure, thus justifying a high success fee. This was puzzling in view of the very good success rate of personal injury cases (Yarrow, 1997).

Further research on the outcome of these cases showed that solicitors did indeed under-estimate the chances of success in a large proportion of cases. Ninety-three per cent of all cases were successful, suggesting that much lower success fees would have been more appropriate. On a more positive note, solicitors did universally adopt the voluntary 25% cap on the proportion of damages that they would take. This therefore constituted a useful safeguard for consumers' interests. Solicitors also did not always take the full success fee to which they were entitled.

Qualitative research with solicitors also showed wide variations in the method used to assess the risk in a case and set the success fee. Some solicitors did not even attempt to relate the success fee to risk, but set a standard success fee, which could be as much as the maximum 100%. They relied on the 25% cap on the percentage of damages as the primary or sole means of setting the success fee. This approach results in a contingency-type fee, based on a percentage of damages. The previous Government had ruled out contingency fees on the basis that they created a greater conflict of interest for lawyers than CFAs. However, the initial regulation of CFAs did not prevent lawyers, in practice, using this type of arrangement. Simultaneously, some solicitors continued offering speculative fees, with no success fee, in very strong cases. A number of different charging systems therefore co-existed. However, this gave no real choice to consumers because they lacked sufficient awareness of the different options.

Research amongst clients showed that their understanding of CFAs was generally very poor. Two out of the forty interviewed did not realise that they would have to pay a success fee at all. Clients often thought that their solicitor would be paid regardless of the outcome of the case, because they thought that the after-the-event insurance would pay their own legal fees if they lost (rather than their opponent's). They did not, therefore, grasp the basic principle of CFAs. Clients did not understand that the success fee could vary and that it was supposed to relate to the risks of the case. One reason for their poor understanding was that the information provided to clients by solicitors needed improvement. The conditional fee agreement, which set out the terms of the contract between solicitor and client, was complicated and difficult to understand. There was very little evidence of price competition on success fees. Clients did not shop around between solicitors; amongst other reasons, they did not appreciate that another firm might quote a lower success fee (Yarrow and Abrams, 1999).

Despite these flaws in the operation of the market, clients were generally satisfied with the success fee, often commenting that it was less than expected. This is partly because their expectations were not always accurate. They might have scrutinised the success fee more closely if they had understood that it was supposed to reflect the chances of success in their case. There was no evidence of clients asking for success fees to be reviewed by the courts (Yarrow and Abrams, 1999).

The initial regulatory framework, therefore, did not protect claimants' interests sufficiently strongly. The Government used the Access to Justice Act 1999 to address these weaknesses and shift the balance in the claimant's favour. From 1 April, defendants have to pay the element in the success fee which reflects the risk of the case being lost. If they do not believe the success fee is reasonable, they can challenge it in court. Defendants in personal injury cases are generally insurance companies who are experienced litigants. They are far more able to look after their interests than are claimants. The Law Society has now removed the 25% cap on the percentage of damages that can be taken by the solicitor, on the grounds that the client no longer needs this protection. New statutory regulation also provides for clients to receive better information. The Law Society has revised its model conditional fee agreement. It now explains how the success fee was calculated although the purpose of this measure is more to enable the solicitor to justify the fee to the court, if challenged, than for the benefit of the claimant. The impact of this remodelling of the CFA scheme has yet to be evaluated.

These changes will, however, not alter the other main principal-agent problem. This is the potential conflict of interest of client and lawyer when a decision is made on whether to settle or to drop the case. Professional self-regulation attempts to address this difficulty by ruling that solicitors should always put the interests of their client first. This potential conflict, present in litigation generally, is magnified in a CFA case. Where payment is dependent on success, in order to be sure of being paid, or be paid quickly, it might be the solicitor's interest to accept a low amount. The existence of the after-the-event insurer also creates a further theoretical conflict of interest. The insurer has a financial interest in a successful outcome, in order to avoid a pay-out on the policy. The after-the-event insurer can potentially influence decisions, because the solicitor must consult them before rejecting an offer to settle. They can withdraw cover for the case if the client does not accept. They have some leverage over solicitors. In 1999, Accident Line Protect threatened to stop lawyers offering their policies if they did not achieve an adequate success rate, usually quoted as 95%.

This is a subject on which is difficult to gather empirical evidence. However, it was clear from the research with clients that, as in much other research on the subject (eg Harris et al, 1984; Law Commission, 1994), solicitors strongly influence clients' expectations and decisions. Clients accepted their solicitors' advice on what were reasonable damages, whether to settle and the costs and benefits of going to trial. As one said: "I'm not all that intelligent, you know, so I go along with things for a quiet life….I've got every faith in [solicitor]. If she said to me tomorrow 'Accept it', then I would". They had little or no other sources of advice. There was no evidence that solicitors had under-settled, but clients would have been unlikely to recognise it if this was the case. The clients' lack of understanding of the financial incentives in CFAs makes them more vulnerable to exploitation.

Access to Justice

As noted above, one of the most important aims of CFAs is to extend access to justice. It is not easy to assess to what extent they have achieved this goal. First, it is not straightforward to measure people's needs for legal services and the degree to which they are being met. Second, the cost of legal advice is only one factor determining whether people bring a claim. Indeed, research shows that only one per cent of people who had taken no action about a personal injury said that they had not done so because of cost (Genn, 1999). There are other barriers such as lack of knowledge that a legal remedy to a problem exists. Third, many other changes are taking place in the legal system which could affect the likelihood of people making a claim. It is difficult to disentangle the impact of CFAs from these. For example, if the current reforms to the civil procedure rules make legal action cheaper and quicker, this might encourage claims. On the other hand, increased court fees may deter litigation in some types of case. Fourth, new providers of legal services are transforming the market in the personal injury field. This is discussed further below.

The impact of CFAs on access to justice is likely to vary for different socio-economic groups. The clients interviewed during the qualitative research on CFAs mainly fell into the middle-income category at whom CFAs were initially targeted. They did feel that CFAs enabled them to bring a claim when they would not otherwise have been able to do so. CFAs also allowed clients to continue with a case which they might have abandoned when their own funds run out. As one said: "I thought it was a wonderful thing. I mean it gives somebody the opportunity to use a solicitor and go for something". (Yarrow & Abrams, 1999). In the survey of solicitors using CFAs, in 76% of cases, solicitors said clients had no other means of funding legal costs. (Yarrow, 1997).

However, this evidence should not be taken at face value. Clients and solicitors may not have been accurate in their perception that they had no other options. Clients relied on solicitors to explain funding methods and had a poor knowledge of other alternatives. There was evidence that solicitors did not fully investigate other funding possibilities such as whether clients already had legal expenses insurance or could get trade union funding. It may not be in solicitors' interests to do so, as the trade union or legal expenses insurer may have arrangements with another solicitor's firm to handle such cases. Clients showed no awareness of the existence of the unofficial version of CFAs, speculative fees. A proportion of the cases funded by CFAs would have gone ahead anyway using speculative fees, although it is not known how many. Clients would not have had to pay a success fee with speculative fees

There are limitations to the extent to which the market will be prepared to provide access. Lawyers limit their commercial risk by restricting the cases that they will accept on a CFA basis. There is evidence that they are risk-averse, despite the potentially greater rewards of a high success fee in cases with poorer prospects of success. Certain types of case are less attractive, for example, if they require an initial costly investment of time, in order to investigate the prospects of success (eg industrial diseases cases). Cases with low damages may not generate a sufficiently high success fee. Even if the firm initially accepts a case, the contract with the client allows it to drop the case later if unfavourable new evidence emerges. After-the-event insurers also wish to limit their exposure to risk. They can either refuse to insure a risky case, or where ability to offer cover is delegated to solicitors, they can exert pressure on them to select only sure-fire cases.

Another potential limitation is that the CFA scheme has not, in the past, completely covered the client's costs. While clients do not pay legal fees, they may have to pay disbursements (eg the cost of reports written by medical or other experts), court fees, and a barrister's fee. These can amount to several hundred pounds, or more in expensive cases. There is also the insurance premium to be paid. When the scheme started, the Accident Line Protect premium was a fairly modest £85 for all types of personal injury case. Premiums have since escalated. At the time of writing, the cheapest policy, for a road traffic accident case in the fast track (ie cases with damages of up to £15,000) is now £300. The most expensive policy, for an occupational diseases case in the multi-track (ie a claim worth £15,000 or more), costs £2,900. The CFA clients interviewed in the study, by definition, had not been deterred by these costs. However, the insurance premium was lower at that time. The costs had caused financial difficulties to a few of them. Clients were concerned about that they would make litigation difficult or impossible for others on lower incomes.

Despite these limitations, CFAs probably have increased the number of personal injury claims brought by people in middle-income groups for a number of reasons. First, the ability to charge an extra success fee is an incentive for lawyers to undertake CFAs. Second, the official sanction for payment by results may encourage lawyers to offer such arrangements. Third, CFAs also appear to have been one catalyst to lawyers stepping up advertising of their personal injury work, which may have stimulated the number of claims. Last, the development of after-the-event insurance accompanying CFAs removes financial risk from clients, making litigation more attractive to them.

The Government's assumption, however, that CFAs will be an adequate substitute for legal aid for people on low incomes is unproven as yet. As indicated above, not all cases are commercially viable. The additional costs of bringing a claim, such as disbursements, may put CFAs out of reach of those in low income groups. The Government's proposals to remove legal aid, which were controversial as they stood, would have been harder to defend had Accident Line Protect insurance premiums been at their current level.

In response to criticisms, the Government has retained some public funding for investigative costs and disbursements and will also fund cases with very high overall costs. But this funding will pay only the excess once expenditure exceeds certain thresholds. These have been set at such high levels that only a small fraction of cases will qualify. Cases must also meet cost-benefit criteria in order to get support.

The Government's assumption is that solicitors will pay the costs not covered by this limited public funding. This will require a major shift in business practice for firms. Not all may be able to afford to sink money into financing personal injury claims in the expectation of future reward. It is also relying on the financial services' industry to fund litigation through insurance and loans. Schemes are available where the insurance premium is not paid until the end of the case, and then only if successful. The premium in winning cases is then normally recovered from the defendant. However, it is not clear whether commercial funding arrangements will provide the same coverage that was available under legal aid. One major firm, for example, launched a scheme to pay for claimants' insurance, but it is aimed primarily at road traffic accidents, which have the highest success rate. The scheme does not cover clinical negligence, complex personal injury claims or industrial diseases (Solicitors' Journal, July 7, 2000).

Impact on legal services market

The loss of legal aid and increasing dependency on CFA income will have an impact on solicitors' firms. Personal injury litigation has been fairly dependent on legal aid funding. In 1999, firms reported that 44% of personal injury claims were funded by legal aid, compared with only 10% by CFAs (Sidaway,1999). The switch to CFAs will affect cash flow. With legal aid, firms received interim payments. With CFAs, they must wait for payment until cases settle, which can take years. Some firms may feel that personal injury work is no longer commercially viable, particularly if they have to cover the escalating cost of insurance premiums and disbursements for clients. The impact of having to finance CFAs is likely to be greatest on small firms. The number of firms offering a personal injury service might fall, reducing rather than increasing competition.

Personal injury is, however, a rapidly changing market. Greater competition is fast emerging – but the impetus is coming from those offering an alternative to the traditional service provided by solicitors. Claims assessors, who are not legally qualified and who charge on a contingency fee basis, are one threat to solicitors' dominance. However, the main competition comes from claims' management firms, which act as intermediaries between the client, solicitor and others such as after-the-event insurers and medical experts (Lord Chancellor's Department, 2000). Claims Direct is the biggest of these firms. Its selling point is that the client does not have to deal with the solicitor or the legal system. Instead, the claims manager smoothes the path. Claims Direct funds clients' insurance premium and disbursements. The company, which was floated on the stock market in July 2000, is spending almost £15 million on TV advertising this year. The main contribution of CFAs to the emergence of this competition is probably in that it enabled the Government to remove legal aid from personal injury. This is a major opportunity for those providing alternative services. Very little is known about how the quality and price of such services compare to those of traditional solicitors. Nor is it known how the level of awards compares.

This phenomenon is having a number of effects. First, solicitors' firms are rapidly joining the panel used by Claims Direct. Firms faced with the loss of legal aid income may have little other option. Second, the legal profession is expanding its own marketing effort, although it may be difficult to compete with Claims Direct's large advertising budget and brand name. Third, solicitors' firms will be under increasing pressure to fund insurance and disbursements, in order to compete. Fourth, Claims Direct's advertising, which emphasises the large sums won by previous clients, is likely to generate not only more claims but perhaps higher expectations of levels of compensation. At the time of the qualitative research with clients, these expectations appeared to be relatively modest but this may change.

Services such as Claims Direct are threatening the legal profession at its weakest point: the perception that it is a baffling and stressful experience to deal with lawyers, and by extension, with the legal system. The fact that it is an attractive option for some people to employ an intermediary in order to avoid dealing with a solicitor directly does not reflect well on the skills of the legal profession. It has yet to be seen whether solicitors' firms will respond to this threat by improving this aspect of their service.*

The market is, therefore, providing additional choice to consumers and is taking advantage of the gap left by the removal of legal aid. However, suppliers are likely to be competing for the pool of profitable low-risk, straightforward cases. There is considerable room for growth in this particular pool. Over one in three people with an injury or health problem resulting from an accident or poor working conditions take no action about it at all (Genn, 1999). However, people who have a case which is meritorious but which does not fit the standard low-risk, straightforward model may not be able to get redress. The full effects of the loss of legal aid funding on claimants are as yet unknown.

Nor is it yet known to what degree the money saved by removing legal aid from personal injury will actually benefit other social priorities through the new Community Legal Service. The savings are relatively modest; the cost of funding personal injury litigation was estimated, according to 1996/7 figures, at £35 million, only 2.5% of a legal aid budget of £1.6 billion. This litigation does not just benefit the individuals concerned. The compensation won enables the State to reduce funding of welfare benefits and health and social care. It is also well-established that litigation can provide public benefits (externalities); in the case of personal injury, it is a means of ensuring employers and others maintain public health and safety. If serious claims are less likely to be pursued, this could have a damaging impact.

Despite some grandiose claims by the Government for the ability of CFAs to transform civil litigation, there is still considerable doubt about their widespread viability outside the confines of personal injury. This area of law has

---

* Recent resistance by defendants regarding the payment of "after the event" insurance premiums to successful claimants has cast a cloud over the prospects of services such as Claims Direct.

characteristics which makes it commercially attractive to both lawyers and after-the-event insurers: cases have a high success rate and outcomes are relatively easy to predict. There is little evidence of extensive use so far in other areas of law. Their viability depends on after-the-event insurers underwriting policies at affordable prices. They have not shown great interest in other areas of law with lower success rates.

References

Bowles, R. (1996). 'Reform of legal aid and the solicitors' profession', *Access to Justice*, Hume Papers on Public Policy **4** (4): Edinburgh University Press.

Genn, H. (1999). *Paths to Justice. What people think and do about going to law.* Oxford: Hart Publishing.

Harris D. et al (1984). *Compensation and Support for Accident and Injury.* Oxford: Clarendon Press

Hilborne N. (2000) 'Irwin Mitchell launches first 'totally free' scheme', *Solicitors' Journal*, (July), **144** (26).

Law Commission (1994). *Personal Injury Compensation. How Much is Enough?* Law Commission, London.

Lord Chancellor's Department (1995). *Legal Aid – Targeting Need.*

Lord Chancellor's Department (1996). *Striking the Balance.*

Lord Chancellor's Department (1997). *More Access to Justice Not Less Says Lord Chancellor*, Press Release 243/97 (October).

Lord Chancellor's Department (2000). *The investigation of non-legally qualified claims assessors and employment advisers who act for reward. (The Blackwell Report)*, (February).

Scottish Legal Aid Board (1999). *Legal aid reform for Scotland welcomed by Scottish Legal Aid Board*, Press Release, (February).

Scottish Office (1998). *McLeish outlines proposed reforms to Scotland's civil legal aid system.* News Release 645/98, (March).

Sidaway, J. (1999). *Surveying Legal Aid Firms.* Paper given to the Legal Aid Board Research Unit Conference, (November), London.

Yarrow, S. & Abrams, P. (1999). *Nothing to Lose. Clients' experiences of using conditional fees. Interim Report*, London: University of Westminster.

Yarrow, S. (1997). *The Price of Success. Lawyers, clients and conditional fees.* London: Policy Studies Institute.

Disclosure, Experts and Information in Litigation*

Paul Fenn, Alastair Gray and Neil Rickman

Introduction

Legal cases often begin with both parties having views (based on private information) about their prospects. To the extent that their information (and interpretations of it) differ from one another's, it may prove difficult or costly to resolve the dispute. Arguably, the litigation process (i.e. the procedures governing litigation) seeks to provide a continual opportunity for parties to transfer information to each other, thereby supposedly aiding settlement prospects. Such opportunities can be formal (such as those provided by disclosure of documents) or informal (such as those provided by responses to settlement offers). With recent policy interest in Scotland (Cullen, 1995), and England and Wales (Woolf, 1996) focusing on reducing the costs and delay of litigation, it is unfortunate that little research has focused on the use, and effects, of such mechanisms. The aim of this paper is to begin such analysis. It does this by examining the use of two important procedural devices that should aid information revelation (disclosure and expert evidence) in a sample of negligence cases (largely medical ones) brought against NHS Trusts between 1978 and 1998. The intention is to present a picture of the extent to which information does flow in such cases and to provide tentative interpretations of the effects it has.

The paper is structured as follows. The next section explains why we focus on disclosure and expert evidence. The discussion here considers the economist's view of the role that such devices can play in producing information. The third section then describes our data before the fourth one presents our analysis of these data. This section contains both descriptive detail on the use of our chosen procedures, and statistical analysis of their effects on settlement probabilities. We perform the latter analysis in order to ask whether the transfer of

---

* Paper originally presented at the Resolution of Legal Disputes Conference, The David Hume Institute, University of Edinburgh; 30 May, 2000. We are grateful for comments received at the conference.

information does, indeed, aid settlement as suggested above. The final section concludes and discusses our results.

Law and information disclosure in economic theory

Economists typically evaluate outcomes relative to a world of certainty and, generally, this means that information deficits (in any setting) can lead to suboptimal outcomes. For example, a lack of information can cause activities to take longer, can cause them to be performed at higher cost and/or can mean that trades do not take place in circumstances where fully informed parties would find mutual benefit in trading. This provides one explanation of how trials come about: they are the result of the parties being unable to resolve their differences because they are unsure about their bargaining strength relative to their opponent's (e.g. Bebchuk, 1984; Reinganum and Wilde, 1986).

From this perspective, the litigation process is one that can be designed to transfer information between the parties, in order to approximate the world of certainty in which most disputes would be resolved. Given the variety of ways in which such information transfer might take place, why focus on formal disclosure and expert witnesses? Apart from the inherent interest of looking at case events that have received little previous attention (Shepherd, 1999), one answer to this question lies in the predictions from economic theory about the effects that formal disclosure may have.

One strand of literature here asks why information disclosure rules are necessary at all. Hay (1994) observes that the threat of 'adverse inference' should be enough to induce parties to release their private information.[1] Thus, if both parties are aware that the defendant possesses certain information that is likely to come out at trial, the plaintiff will 'assume the worst' about this information if it is not revealed. Accordingly, defendants whose information is unfavourable but not excessively so will release their information. Of course, the plaintiff can be predicted to anticipate that only weaker defendants will not have released their information, and adjust his negotiation strategy accordingly. Defendants with intermediately weak cases will feel obliged to reveal their information, and so on. This 'unravelling process' finally stops when all defendants have revealed their information, without the need for discovery rules.

The fact that we do observe disclosure rules indicates that unravelling is not expected to work on all occasions. As Hay notes, the obvious example of this will be information that the opponent is unaware of and whose non-disclosure cannot, therefore, lead to any adverse inference. Such information can (literally) be discovered via the discovery process.

Thinking carefully about the implications of this analysis it seems that disclosure need not, unambiguously, improve the speed of settlements. This is because one can expect it to transfer information that weakens its owner and,

---

[1] Of course, this remark relates to the parties' unfavourable private information. It seems likely that they will release favourable material without procedural inducement.

conversely, strengthens its recipient. To the extent that a stronger opponent bargains harder, settlement may actually be delayed.

Other authors have indicated ways in which discovery can aid settlement. Shavell (1989)[2] for example considers a setting where a party (say, plaintiffs) can reveal their private information on the damages they have suffered before the start of the case. He considers two scenarios: one where plaintiffs can credibly reveal their information and another in which some cannot. In the former model, discovery does nothing to the probability of trial because all plaintiffs settle. The reasoning is that, for a given settlement offer from the defendant to all possible 'types' of plaintiff (a 'pooling offer'), low-damage plaintiffs will accept this while high damage ones reveal their true types and receive appropriate separating offers. The only role for (costless) discovery here is to remove the need for the pooling settlement offer (thereby extracting 'information rent' from the silent plaintiffs).

In Shavell's second model, discovery increases the probability of settlement. The reason is that there will be some badly damaged plaintiffs who find the available pooling offer unacceptable. However, being unable to reveal their types, they cannot extract a more acceptable offer from their opponent. In this situation, allowing the defendant to see the information of those who can credibly convey it will raise the pooling settlement offer and increase settlement. This is because discovery allows the defendant to screen out those low-damage plaintiffs who remained silent in the hope of receiving a high pooling offer. This raises the average damages amongst the (genuinely) silent plaintiffs and therefore raises the settlement offer.

In this second case, therefore, information can speed settlement. Note, however, that the situation is different from Hay's. In Shavell's model, plaintiffs with favourable information may be unable to transmit it. As a result, discovery gives them a mechanism for separating themselves from others with poor information (who can transmit it) and, therefore informs the defendant that her opponent is strong. The result is speedier settlement. The choice between these two sets of predictions, therefore, depends on whether it is more likely that some parties cannot credibly convey 'good' information (Shavell) or that others will attempt to conceal 'bad' information that the plaintiff is unaware of (Hay).[3]

So far, we have discussed the transfer of private information between the parties. However, it seems feasible that the litigation process may also produce information that neither party has at the start of the case and which is beneficial to both of them. Several examples are possible. Experts in medical negligence cases may produce a prognosis upon which both sides are waiting; an interim decision (by the court or a legal expert) may clarify both parties' positions; relevant precedent may be set elsewhere. The key features of such

---

[2] See also Cooter and Rubinfeld (1994).
[3] Another possibility is that parties use disclosure as a (wasteful) strategic device, to heap costs onto the opponent, not all of which (including the 'hassle' involved) may be recoverable. The current paper does not analyse this possibility but it is clearly important future research.

information are that it is objective (i.e. it is provided impartially) and that both sides know that the other has received it (so they can predict its effects on their opponent). In order to contrast this information with the 'private' information described above, we refer to it from now on as 'public information'. Cooter and Rubinfeld (1994) refer briefly to such information and suggest that it should speed settlement because it resolves some residual uncertainty for both parties. Fenn, Gray and Rickman (2000) show, however, that this need not be the case: the outcome depends on the precise nature of the public information.

Thus, we have a number of predictions about how different forms of information will affect litigation. In Section 4, we try to shed light on which (if any of these) appear to characterise the roles of information disclosure in our data.

Data

To consider the extent to which the litigation process transfers information between the litigants we use a database of claims brought against a group of NHS Trusts in England and Wales.[4] Of these claims, roughly 80% were medical negligence cases and 20% were employee claims. The data on existing cases are regularly updated and new ones are added. The full database consists of 2,691 cases settled or abandoned between 1978 and 1998 although, on occasions, we use the 734 settled or abandoned between 1990 and 1995. (This allows us to focus on closed claims and to avoid any 'Woolf anticipation effect'.)

The strength of the data for current purposes is their rich variety of claim-specific data. In particular, we have information on the initiation date, the closure date, defence costs (and plaintiff costs proxied by the degree of cost exposure afforded by the plaintiff's fee arrangements, where known), damages paid (if any), the defence's prior estimate of liability and case severity (along with updates on these) and the use of a variety of procedural devices (e.g. discovery, expert witness reports, payment-in).

Table 1 contains basic descriptive data about the cases in our sample. As can be seen from Table 1, total delay from incidence to closure was approximately 2,000 days (5 years): this reflects the acknowledged fact that medical negligence cases tend to take longer than other personal injury claims on average. Of these cases, some 26% settled with payment to the plaintiff and this (including plaintiff's costs) averaged £21,465. Defence costs were roughly 10% of this.

Analysis

The defendant's perceptions about the case

In this section, we consider the extent to which the defendant's (i.e. the Trusts' claims handlers') views about the case change over time. This, presumably,

---

[4] Thus, the data are collected from defendants' case files. See Fenn, Gray and Rickman (1999) and Fenn and Rickman (1999) for more detail.

Table 1

	Mean	Std. Deviation
Delay from incident to claim (days)	1066	1835
Delay from claim to closure (days)	1004	759
Settled with payment (%)	25.9	43.8
Damages paid to plaintiff inc costs (£)	21465	71718
Defence costs (£)	2209	7957
Payments to expert witnesses (£)	286	1505
Payments to counsel (£)	254	2104

is an indicator of whether the defendant learns as the case progresses and, if so, whether the learning improves or harms his case. As the defendant's expected pay-out to the plaintiff is the product of estimated quantum and liability, we focus chiefly on these. Tables 2 and 3 indicate how these change through the case with the former looking at quantum and the latter looking at liability.

From Table 2, we see that the defendant's views about the financial sums at stake do change over time: anticipated quantum rises by £8,000, while own and opponent's costs almost double. In the case of costs, this reflects the fact that cases where such revisions are necessary must be accumulating costs over time. As far as quantum is concerned, the table suggest that cases taking longer to be resolved (i.e. needing such revisions) are found to be more serious with the passage of time: perhaps they need time for the full extent of an injury to become apparent.

The nature of quantum revisions over time is also revealed by Figure 1. This shows the average estimate of claim value depending on the year of settlement. It can be seen that cases settling quickly (three years) appear to do so because the defendant's position strengthens: her estimate of quantum falls. This is not true, however, of case taking longer than three years to settle. In each case, the defendant becomes more pessimistic about quantum with each passing year. This effect is particularly striking with cases lasting six years: here, the final year sees the defendant substantially revising estimated quantum upwards. It seems clear that such cases are delayed because the parties need time to learn about the plaintiff's injuries – or, at least, the defendant needs to correct an earlier (perhaps mistaken) belief that the plaintiff is not seriously hurt. Table 3 tells us that similar information becomes apparent on liability. As can be seen,

Table 2

	Mean	Std. Deviation
Initial estimate of damages	40783	137719
Final estimate of damages	48854	183647
Initial estimate of own costs	1436	4561
Final estimate of own costs	2597	8298
Initial estimate of third party costs	1960	6210
Final estimate of third party costs	4194	11911

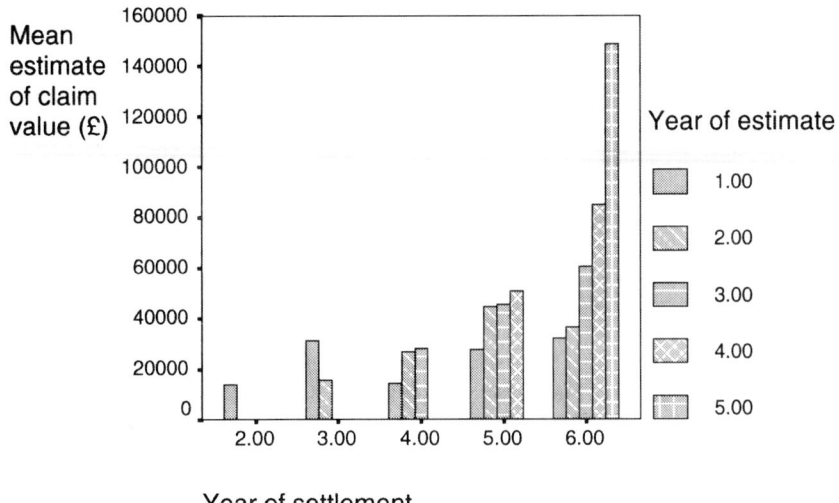

Figure 1

the defendant begins the case with a reasonably even spread of opinions as to whether she will be able to defend the claim. The largest percentage, however, is the 40% of cases where no clear estimate can be made initially. As the case proceeds these 'unclear' cases resolve themselves fairly evenly between 'liable' and 'not liable' (percentages for other categories remain quite stable). Again, therefore, we have evidence of learning taking place as the case develops: in the current table, this involves the defendant discovering more about the appropriateness of its actions in the case.

Table 3

	First estimate		Last estimate	
	Frequency	Valid Percent	Frequency	Valid Percent
liable	217	9.3	391	17.2
probably liable	32	1.4	21	0.9
poorly defensible	233	10.0	229	10.1
probably defensible	305	13.1	371	16.3
defensible	193	8.3	177	7.8
probably not liable	35	1.5	27	1.2
not liable	253	10.8	521	22.9
unclear	926	39.6	397	17.5
missing	143	6.1	140	6.2
Total	2337	100.0	2274	100.0

Table 4

	N	Minimum	Maximum	Mean	Std. dev.
Time to expert report	293	1	3,560	667.56	571.37
Time to disclosure	882	2	2,628	119.18	215.16

Effects of procedures

Next, we consider the effects of two procedural devices: disclosure of documents and use of expert witnesses. Recalling our earlier discussion, these will be our proxies for mechanisms for transferring 'private' information and 'public' information respectively.

Table 4 shows the incidence of these activities in our 2,691 cases (1974–1998) and the speed with which they take place. It is apparent that we have roughly one-third as many observations of expert reports (293) as we do document disclosure (882).[5] However, the time leading up to expert reports is between five and six times as long (667 days against 119 days): thus, disclosure takes place within four months of the claim being filed, on average, while expert reports take an average of two years to arrive. This is consistent with the need for experts to assess the case and, in particular, the seriousness of the plaintiff's injuries before producing a report.

Our theoretical discussion suggested a possible link between the role played by these procedural events and the probability of settling the case. Of course, many other factors may also affect this probability so we need to control for these when assessing the effects of interest to us. Accordingly, we now present econometric analysis of the 734 claims in our sample that were settled or abandoned between 1990 and 1995. In particular, we focus on the determinants of the 'conditional probability' of settling the case once a claim has been initiated. This calculates the probability of settlement at time t given that the case has not closed prior to this point. An increase in this conditional probability implies a reduction in delay from time t onwards: there is now more likelihood of settlement. The particular advantage of this approach for us is that it allows us to look at how procedural events affect the settlement probability conditional on such an event having taken place. This is exactly where the earlier theory focused.

Table 5 presents our results.[6] It shows the effects of variables ranging from initial defence estimates of case value, costs and liability to the role of injury severity, procedural events and the nature of the plaintiff's funding arrangements (where known to the defendant). Two sets of results are given: one excluding changes in defendant beliefs (on quantum and liability) as a variable

---

[5] Of course, such activities may also have taken place in other cases but not been recorded in the database.

[6] In Table 5, an entry by the side of a variable indicates statistical significance. The direction of this significance is denoted by a '+' (meaning that a rise in the variable in question increases delay) or a '−' (meaning that a rise in the variable in question decreases delay). The complete set of results is available from the authors on request.

Table 5

Variable	Impact on settlement delay (where significant)	
	Without Δ beliefs	With Δ beliefs
• the defendant's initial estimate of case value	+	+
• the defendant's initial estimate of incremental defence costs	–	–
• the defendant's initial estimate of incremental plaintiff costs		–
• the defendant's initial estimate of its liability	–	–
• the severity of plaintiff's injury (as known to the defendant):		
• insignificant		–
• temporary minor		
• temporary major		
• permanent partial minor		+
• permanent partial major	+	+
• permanent total	+	
• death		
• procedural events:		
• disclosure	+	~+
• explanatory letter		
• receipt of expert's report	–	~
• receipt of witness statement		+
• initiation of legal proceedings (writ served)		–
• offer of settlement	–	
• payment into court	–	–
• trial date	–	–
• changes in beliefs:		
• defendant's estimate if case value	n/a	+
• defendant's estimate of liability	n/a	–
• the source of plaintiff finance (relative to "not known"):		
• legal aid	–	–
• trade union	–	–
• private finance	–	–

explaining settlement probability, the other including these changes. We return to these below.

First, consider the results excluding changes in beliefs. Many of these are intuitive. Thus, all other things equal, higher value cases (both in the defendant's estimation and in terms of the nature of the plaintiff's injury) increase delay (they reduce the conditional probability of settlement) while higher cost cases lower delay. Apparently, the parties are keen to avoid cost and they do this by settling early. However, in high value cases where the plaintiff is badly injured, the parties need time to reach agreement.[7] It is interesting, and understandable, that permanent injuries have the most significant impact on delay.

Moving to the bottom of Table 5, we find 'plaintiff finance'. These results

---

[7] A possible explanation for this is that they need to learn about the case prognosis. Farber and White (1991; 1994), however, also observe that a hospital may 'sit back' and wait to see whether plaintiffs choose to pursue larger valued cases: effectively, the hospital may screen such plaintiffs for their litigiousness (i.e. their appetite for litigation).

show how the means by which the plaintiff is funded affects settlement timing. Three possibilities are considered, relative to cases where the means of plaintiff finance are 'unknown' in the database. Legal aid, trade union finance and private finance all reduce delay relative to the 'unknown' category. However, it is apparent that private finance does this by more than trade union finance which, in turn reduces delay by more than legal aid. Fenn and Rickman (1999) rationalise these results by noting that the expense of a large medical negligence case will be a significant disincentive to self-funded litigants and, to a lesser extent, to third party funders who carefully monitor case activity (e.g. trade unions). However, such monitoring may have been less strict in legally aided cases (Gray, Fenn and Rickman, 1996) with the result that plaintiffs and their solicitors were insulated against the costs of (many) decisions.

The middle of Table 5 presents results on the impact of 'procedural events'. Here we find that disclosure of documents increases delay while experts' reports, settlement offers, payment-into-court and trial dates all speed up the case, *ceteris paribus*. It seems correct that the offer of a settlement amount should stimulate settlement. Similarly, a number of authors have suggested that payment-in will do this by shifting bargaining power to the defendant (see Main and Park, 2000), and Spier (1992) shows that the setting down of a trial date creates a 'deadline effect' by concentrating minds on the possibility of a costly trial.

The effects of disclosure and expert reports can be assessed in the light of our theory. The fact that disclosure increases settlement delay is consistent with our interpretation of Hay's argument, that parties will seek to conceal unfavourable information when adverse inference is unlikely.[8] In turn, being allowed to find such information strengthens the plaintiff and stiffens his negotiating position. By contrast, expert reports appear to reduce settlement delay. This, again, is consistent with the earlier theory, where we suggested that such reports may generate 'public' information that is helpful to both parties. In Cooter and Rubinfeld's (1994) terms, the resolution of common uncertainty eases settlement negotiations. Thus, our results are consistent with two types of information being produced, and transmitted, by the litigation process.

One difficulty with these results is that they do not specify clearly the mechanisms by which our chosen procedural devices affect litigation. For example, rather than conveying information, such events may simply have strategic impacts on litigants. In order to begin understanding this, the second column of Table 5 includes an extra set of regressors: the changes in defendant beliefs about liability and quantum. The reasoning behind including these is that, if our procedural events convey genuinely new information, they should affect

---

[8] One obstacle to this interpretation is that, when the database lists the documents discovered, it often refers to "patients' notes". It seems highly unlikely that patients would be unaware of these and, accordingly, that no adverse inference would be drawn if they were withheld. One possibility is that some features of a medical record may be sufficiently technical that patients (or their solicitors) would not anticipate them. Clearly, the precise details of the information disclosed at discovery warrants further study.

beliefs and, in this way, affect negotiating positions. This is what we find. Changes in beliefs have significant effects on settlement timing with increases in beliefs over quantum increasing delay and increases in beliefs over liability reducing delay: defendants clearly seek to 'cut their losses' once confident they will lose. Importantly, however, although most other results are robust to these new variables, those for disclosure and expert reports are not. In each case, they lose their statistical significance. One interpretation of this is that, once the *effects* of these activities are explicitly incorporated (i.e. the changes in beliefs), the activities themselves are no longer important. This appears to strengthen the suggestion that information is flowing as a result of these activities.

Conclusions

An important function played, in principle, by the litigation process is the production and transfer of information between litigants. However, the very nature of this process has made it difficult for researchers to examine the extent to which this happens in practice, or indeed the extent to which it takes place. The aim of this paper has been to provide such analysis using a rich set of data from cases brought against NHS Trusts in a particular region. The analysis suggests a good deal of learning (at least by the defendants we observe) as a case proceeds, with views on liability and quantum changing over time and, on occasions, affecting settlement timing. Our results also seem to suggest that different procedural devices (discovery and experts) may have different effects on settlement, despite both being aimed at improving information available to the parties. One interpretation of this is that the two procedures are producing different types of information: whereas discovery transfers private information (and may, therefore make settlement harder to achieve), experts produce new information for both sides ('public information'). Of course, such conclusions are preliminary and simply recommend an avenue for further research.

Our results can be placed in the context of recent policy debate. The place of discovery and experts in civil litigation came in for much discussion during Lord Woolf's consultation on procedural reform in England and Wales during the 1990s. The former was regarded as inefficient and disproportionate to the value of many (particularly larger) cases, while the latter was also considered time-consuming. Indeed, Lord Woolf questioned the need for parties to engage their own experts and (in his Interim Report: Woolf, 1995) suggested that the court should appoint experts rather than the parties. Although this final suggestion attracted criticism (and does not appear in Woolf, 1996) his final proposals suggest that only one expert should be required in most cases. If our interpretation of the role of experts in our medical negligence data is correct, it may support this view: a single expert (with suitable allegiance to the court, rather than to one of the parties) may well be able to produce the kind of 'public information' we have conjectured upon in this paper.

Having said this, it is noticeable that, in general, Lord Woolf's reform proposals are not the product of detailed analysis of the effects and uses of the procedural devices we have analysed. While one may not disagree with the costs he identified, they should be set against any benefits that might accrue due to the process of information transfer they appear to support. We hope that the current paper takes some early steps towards providing this more detailed analysis and suggesting some paths for further research. The importance (and interest) of the area, to policymakers and researchers alike, will hopefully do the rest.

References

Bebchuk, L. (1984). "Litigation and Settlement Under Imperfect Information", *RAND Journal of Economics*, **15**: 404–415.

Cooter, R. & Rubinfeld, D. (1994). "An Economic Model of Legal Discovery", *Journal of Legal Studies*, **23**: 435–463.

Cullen, Lord D.(1995). *Review of the business of the Outer House of the Court of Session*. Edinburgh: Scottish Courts Administration.

Farber, H. & White, M. (1991). "Medical Malpractice: An Empirical Examination of the Litigation Process", *RAND Journal of Economics*, **22**: 199–217.

Farber, H. & White, M. (1994). "A Comparison of Formal and Informal Dispute Resolution in Medical Malpractice", *Journal of Legal Studies*, **23**: 777–806.

Fenn, P. & Rickman, N. (1999). "Delay and Settlement in Litigation", *Economic Journal*, **109**: 476–491.

Fenn, P., Gray, A. & Rickman, N. (1999. Forthcoming, "The Impact of Plaintiff Finance on Personal Injury Litigation: An Empirical Analysis", Lord Chancellor's Department Research Series, London.

Fenn, P., Gray, A. & Rickman, N. (2000). "Information Transfer and the Litigation Process", Paper presented at the Annual Conference of the European Association of Law and Economics, Ghent, September.

Gray, A., Fenn, P. & Rickman, N. (1996). "Monitoring Legal Aid: Back to First Principals", *Hume Papers on Public Policy*, **4**: 24–35.

Hay, B. (1994). "Civil Discovery: Its Effects and Optimal Scope", *Journal of Legal Studies*, **23**: 481–515.

Main, B. & Park, A. (2000). "The British and American Rules: an experimental examination of pre-trial bargaining in the shadow of the law", *Scottish Journal of Political Economy*, **47**: 37–60.

Reinganum, J. & Wilde, L. (1986). "Settlement, Litigation and the Allocation of Legal Costs", *RAND Journal of Economics*, **17**: 557–566.

Shavell, S. (1989). "Sharing Information Prior to Settlement or Litigation", *RAND Journal of Economics* **20**: 183–195.

Shepherd, G. (1999). "An Empirical Study of the Economics of Pre-Trial Discovery", *International Review of Law and Economics*, **19**: 245–263.

Spier, K. (1992). "The Dynamics of Pre-trial Negotiation", *Review of Economic Studies*, **59**: 93–108.

Woolf, Lord H. (1995). *Access to Justice: Interim Report to the Lord Chancellor on the Civil Justice System in England and Wales*, London: HMSO.
Woolf, Lord H. (1996). *Access to Justice: Final Report to the Lord Chancellor on the Civil Justice System in England and Wales*, London: HMSO.

Reform of Legal Aid in Scotland*

Frank H Stephen

Legal Aid expenditure has grown enormously in the UK in recent years. Both the Lord Chancellor's Department for England and Wales[1] and the Scottish Office for Scotland[2] have embarked on a process of reform. Rickman, Fenn and Gray (1999) have recently reviewed the position in England and Wales and analysed the proposals for reform of the system in that jurisdiction. The present paper is concerned particularly with recent and proposed reforms to Criminal Legal Aid in Scotland. The first section compares expenditure trends on legal aid in Scotland with those in England, the second examines the Scottish situation in more detail and the third subjects the recent and proposed reforms of Criminal Legal Aid in Scotland to detailed examination.

Legal Aid Expenditure in Scotland and in England and Wales

Expenditure on Legal Aid in Great Britain has grown dramatically in the last twenty years. Table 1 summarises the annual percentage growth in nominal

---

* Comments of participants in the UK Law and Economics Seminar and The David Hume Institute Seminar on Settlement of Legal Disputes are gratefully acknowledged. The author is also grateful to the Law Society of Scotland for a research grant which made some of the work reported here possible. However, the opinions expressed here are those of the author only and any errors are his own.

[1] Since the mid–1990s there has been considerable concern with the growing legal aid bill among policymakers as evidenced by a series of consultation documents and White Papers dealing with alternative contracting mechanisms including the use of conditional fees to replace much of civil legal aid (LCD, 1995, 1996, 1997, 1998a). This has culminated in the Access to Justice Act 1999 which set up the Legal Services Commission to replace the Legal Aid Board and oversee the Community Legal Service for civil legal aid and information and a Criminal Defence Service to be introduced from April 2001.

[2] In Scotland concern has been oriented towards criminal legal aid as evidenced by the introduction of an experimental Public Defence Solicitor Office and the establishing of fixed fees for summary cases in the *Criminal Legal Aid (Fixed Payments) (Scotland) Regulations 1999*.

Table 1. Annual Growth of Legal Aid Expenditure (Percentage)

Period	Growth in Nominal Expenditure		Growth in GDP deflator		Growth in Volume		Growth in Real Expenditure per Case	
	E&W	Sco	E&W	Sco	E&W	Sco	E&W	Sco
1980–85	17.2	16.8	6.7	6.9	11.9	6.7	−1.8	2.5
1985–90	16.0	10.3	5.8	5.6	6.6	10.1	2.8	−5.0
1990–95	15.4	14.5	3.6	3.7	7.4	7.2	3.8	3.0
1980–95	16.2	13.8	5.4	5.4	8.6	8.0	1.6	0.1

E and W: Rickman, Fenn and Gray (1999), Table 3. Scotland: SLAB Annual Reports.

expenditure during each five year period from 1980 to 1995 and for the period as a whole for both jurisdictions. Using a method similar to that used by Rickman, Fenn and Gray (1999) the contribution to the growth in expenditure from inflation, growth in the volume of acts of legal aid and in the average real cost of each act is also shown. The rates of growth have converged in the most recent period. This has continued throughout the 1990s. Expenditure has grown in Scotland from £67.75m in 1990/91 to £145.1m in 1997/98, while in England and Wales it has grown from £682.3m to £1526m over the same period. This suggests a very similar rate of growth in both systems over the period: each more than doubling expenditure in nominal terms and increasing by seventy per cent in real terms.

Despite the fact that public expenditure *per capita* in Scotland is generally above that in England and Wales, *per capita* expenditure on Legal Aid has been very similar in the two jurisdictions as may be seen by comparing the two panels of Chart 1. However, the overall rates of growth for the two systems obscure divergent rates of growth for different elements of each system and between the two systems.

Chart 1 and Table 2 illustrate that the distribution between Civil and Criminal Legal Aid differs between the two countries as do the rates of growth of the two elements. Rickman, Fenn and Gray (1999) illustrate the divergence between the various elements of the Legal Aid system in England and Wales in terms of expenditure growth, volume growth and the growth of expenditure per case over the period since 1980 (Table 4) and for various sub-periods (Table 5). This shows that the highest growth in expenditure has been in civil cases

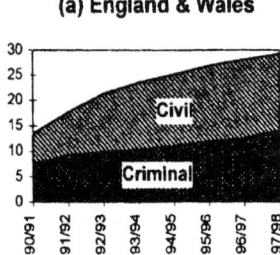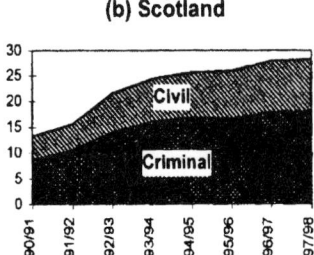

Chart 1. Growth of Legal Aid Expediture 1990/1–1997/8

Table 2. Criminal Legal Aid Expenditure
(Percentage of Total Legal Aid Expenditure)

Year	England & Wales	Scotland
1990/91	56.22%	64.25%
1991/92	52.10%	66.00%
1992/93	46.39%	63.62%
1993/94	43.59%	64.93%
1994/95	43.80%	64.29%
1995/96	44.36%	62.80%
1996/97	44.62%	62.64%
1997/98	48.03%	63.47%

whose volume and average cost have contributed equally. Much of the growth in expenditure on civil cases has taken place in the period 1990–1995. Stephen (1998) presents a similar disaggregation for the Scottish system for the period 1990/1 to 1996/7. However his analysis shows that it has been criminal legal aid that has contributed most to the growth of expenditure in Scotland in recent years.

Expenditure on Criminal Legal Aid declined as a proportion of the total in England and Wales during the first part of the decade but has risen latterly. However, it has been increasing in real terms throughout the period. Expenditure on Civil Legal Aid, however, has increased at a much faster rate. In Scotland the difference between the growth rates for criminal and civil matters is less pronounced over the period. Tables 3 illustrates these points.

The Scottish Legal Aid system remains predominately a system of *criminal* legal aid whilst that in England and Wales has become gradually one of *civil* legal aid. Consequently, until recently, policy innovations in England and Wales have focused on controlling civil legal aid expenditure through *inter alia* switching emphasis towards conditional fees in money cases[3]. In Scotland the emphasis has been on controlling legal aid expenditure through *inter alia* an experimental public defender's office and the introduction of fixed fees for criminal work. The rest of this paper examines the nature of the growth in expenditure in Scotland and assesses the proposals to control it.

Table 3. Growth Rates *per annum* Civil and Criminal Legal Aid Expenditure *per capita*, 1990/1–1997/8

England & Wales	Criminal	9.2%
	Civil	14.5%
Scotland	Criminal	11.0%
	Civil	12.2%

---

[3] Although the major reform of the Legal Aid System in England & Wales initiated with the passage of the Access to Justice Act 1999 involves, inter alia measures to shift criminal legal aid to a block contract basis. A Criminal Defence Service is to be introduced from April 2001.

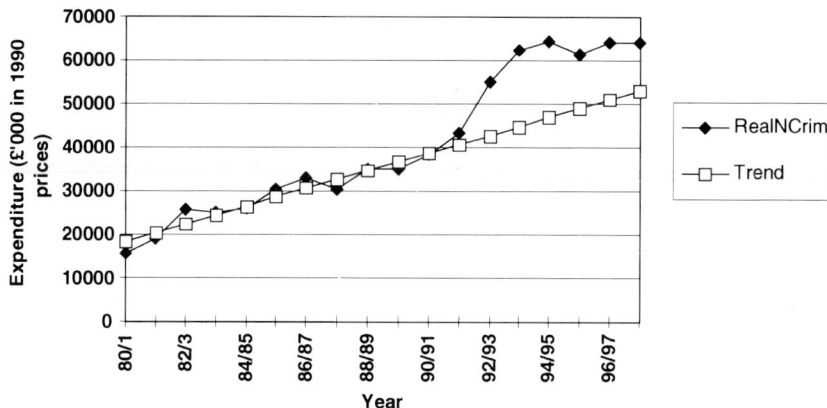

Chart 2. Actual and Trend Real Expenditure on Criminal Legal Aid in Scotland

Criminal Legal Aid in Scotland

Chart 2 shows how real expenditure on criminal legal aid in Scotland has grown since 1980. It also shows what expenditure would have been had the trend rate of growth of the 1980s continued into the 1990s. A dramatic shift from the trend clearly took place in the early 1990s. The source of the change can be more clearly identified by examining the components of the criminal legal aid more closely.

The main component of expenditure on Criminal Legal Aid in Scotland is the Nominated Solicitor Scheme[4] under which defendants may nominate the solicitor of their choice to defend them. In 1997/98 this scheme accounted for just under 96% of expenditure on Criminal Legal Aid and 53.5% of *all* Legal Aid expenditure compared to 98% and 55.3% respectively in 1990/91. Table 4 presents summary information on the Nominated Solicitor Scheme. Over the period 1990/91 to 1997/98 expenditure under the scheme rose by 63% in real terms with the volume of cases paid for rising by 22%.

However, the number of cases in the Sheriff Court[5] grew by 53% from just over 63% of Nominated Solicitor Scheme cases in 1990/91 to over 79% by 1997/98. Goriely *et al* (1997) suggests that in the early 1990s there was a shift in venue of summary trials from the District to Sheriff Court where more severe sentences could be imposed. The implication is that this was a decision of the Crown Office in Edinburgh. It is likely also to have contributed to the increase in expenditure per case under the Nominated Solicitor Scheme. The cost of each Sheriff Court case did, however, rise over the period by 31%.

---

[4] Other schemes are the Duty Solicitor Scheme and the Criminal Appeals Scheme.

[5] In criminal matters three levels of court have jurisdiction in Scotland: High Court, Sheriff Court and District Court. The Sheriff Court corresponds roughly to the Crown Court in England.

Table 4. Nominated Solicitor Scheme 1990/91–1997/98 (Expenditure and cost per case in 1990 prices)

		1990/91	1997/98	Ratio
Nominated Solicitor Scheme	Expenditure	£37.482M	£61.187M	1.63
	Cases	59,888	72,870	1.22
	Cost/Case	£626	£840	1.34
Sheriff Court Cases	Expenditure	£23.090M	£46.202M	2.00
	Cases	37,888	58,038	1.53
	Cost/Case	£609	£798	1.31
Cases without trial in Sheriff Court	Expenditure	£7.497M	£37.784M	5.04
	Cases	17,762	51,554	2.90
	Cost/Case	£422	£733	1.74

Sources: Scottish Legal Aid Board, Annual Report, 1991, 1998

The most dramatic change in expenditure in the Nominate Solicitor Scheme was the increase in cases in the Sheriff Court 'without trial' for which expenditure increased by over 500% in real terms. These are, predominately, cases where the defendant changes plea from 'not guilty' to 'guilty' at (or shortly before) the trial. An accused person charged under summary jurisdiction who pleads guilty is not entitled to full representation under the Nominated Solicitor Scheme of legal aid. Such persons are only entitled to a minimal representation under ABWOR. It has been argued that this leads to accused persons pleading 'not guilty' in order to access legal aid and then changing the plea to 'not guilty' at trial. This issue is discussed more fully in Stephen (1998), Samuel (1996) and Goriely et al (1997).

As Table 4 illustrates 'cases without trial' in the Sheriff Court had more resources expended on them in 1997/98 than all cases under the Nominated Solicitor Scheme in 1990/91. Indeed, this category of cases accounted for 33% of *all expenditure on legal aid* in Scotland in 1997/98 compared to a mere 11% in 1990/91. The average cost of these cases had grown by 74% over this period. The data in Table 4 is transformed into annual growth rates in Table 5.

It is tempting to suggest that there is an element of 'supplier induced demand' lying behind this growth: solicitors inducing defendants to plead not guilty in order to generate fees from the Legal Aid fund that they could not otherwise access. This would be a result of the agency relationship between the solicitor and the Scottish Legal Aid Board (SLAB). However there is another adverse selection problem between the accused person and both the solicitor and SLAB: only the accused person knows his/her guilt or innocence.

Qualitative evidence from in-depth interviews of accused persons and their agents (Samuel, 1996) suggests that accused persons are well aware of the fact that a not guilty plea gives access to careful scrutiny of the strength of Crown evidence, a professionally prepared plea in mitigation and, at worst, a postponement of the 'evil day'. Furthermore, it is likely that the changes in plea may not be to all charges or may represent a guilty plea to a reduced set of charges. The work loads of procurators fiscal[6] do not provide opportunities for

---

[6] The procurators fiscal are the public prosecutors in the sheriff and district courts. They are full-time civil servants …. and are usually solicitors' Manson-Smith (1995).

Table 5. Annual Growth in Criminal Legal Aid Expenditure (percentage)

	Growth in Nominal Expenditure	Growth in GDP Deflator	Growth in Volume	Growth in Cost per Case
Nominated Solicitor Scheme	10.94	3.44	2.84	4.29
Cases in Sheriff Court	14.26	3.44	6.28	3.94
Sheriff Court Cases with No Trial	30.33	3.44	16.44	8.21

plea bargaining prior to the initial plea and solicitors argue that it would be against their clients' interests and a failure in their professional duty to recommend an initial guilty plea in most cases. However, were public funds available for reasonable defence agent preparation, including discussion with the procurator fiscal (representing the Crown), prior to the initial plea it is likely that the rate of guilty pleas would increase, court and prosecution time be saved and a reduction in the burden on legal aid resources obtained.

An alternative explanation of the increasing average cost of criminal legal aid arises from the observation of increasing delays in, and lengthening of, cases in the Scottish criminal courts during the 1990s. Such an explanation would suggest that average costs would rise as the number of criminal cases rose and *vice versa*. Stephen (1998) reports some econometric results which suggest that this explanation is closer to the truth than the 'supplier induced demand' explanation.

Government Proposals for the Reform of Summary Criminal Legal Aid

The Government has come forward with two proposals which it argues will bring public expenditure on criminal legal aid under control: a *Public Defence Solicitors Office* and *fixed fees* for summary Legal Aid. Neither proposal directly addresses the issue of late changes of plea. The next section of this paper examines these proposals in detail.

Public Defence Solicitors

An experimental system of SLAB funded public defenders had been established in Scotland which has operated since the beginning of October 1998[7]. The office consists of six solicitors who will provide defence services in Edinburgh Sheriff and District Courts for accused persons under summary jurisdiction whose birth falls in the months of January and February. This experiment will operate for five years and a report on its effects will have to be laid before the Scottish parliament after three years. It is argued by its

---

[7] A similar provision is possible under the Public Defence Service to be introduced in England & Wales from April 2001.

supporters that direct public employment of defence agents will be more economical because it avoids the potential of 'supplier induced demand' inherent in the fee for service contracts offered under the existing system.

The use of public defence solicitors, at first glance, seems a way of solving the principal-agent problem between the provider and the third-party payer. A public defender appears to have no incentive to over or under-supply services since there is no profit relation involved. However, a principal-agent relationship still exists between the public defender and his/her employer. The employer will have objectives to be met through the employment of the public defender and the question remains how the employee's performance will be judged against these objectives. Performance-related pay or promotion related to performance against objectives are ways of encouraging an employee's efforts to be directed toward the employer's objectives. However, research has shown that this results in employees focusing exclusively on the measurable components of performance. The number of cases dealt with over a specified time period would be a ready measure of a public defence solicitor's performance. However, this could encourage an under-supply of services to each client in order to enhance the 'throughput' of clients. In fact, this results in the public defender responding to incentives in much the same way as a financially motivated independent supplier who is paid a fixed fee by a third party payer (e.g. SLAB).

International evidence is consistent with the above predictions. Goriely (1997) reports that Australian staff (public defence) lawyers have an incentive to get through as many cases as possible (p.42) and are consequently cheaper (p.97). Evidence from Canada suggests that they tend to enter more guilty pleas (Goriely, 1997: 2) and spend more time in plea and sentence bargaining with prosecutors (Goriely, 1997: 23). On the other hand Goriely (1997: 3) suggests that the evidence from Canada is that cheaper service does not necessarily imply a worse service when measured by outcome as clients of staff lawyers were convicted no more often than those of independent lawyers and indeed were less likely to face a prison sentence. After discussing the Australian experience she concludes:

> 'The evidence is that staff lawyers take less long. The questions that need to be explored are whether this is because they handle easy cases to start off with; whether they provide a worse service; or they act more efficiently'. (p.43)

A system of public defence solicitors might also suffer from other disadvantages. The individual public defence solicitor has no incentive to innovate. Furthermore, it is unlikely that every District or Sheriff Court in Scotland will be able to justify full-time public defence solicitors. This will imply the need to continue to use private suppliers, perhaps on a block contract basis. Where there is a mix of public and private supply there will be a need for some mechanism to allocate cases between the public defender and private suppliers.

There is also the question of whether a career as a public defender would be attractive to those solicitors who currently enter private practice and thereafter specialise in criminal work. A career which consists of periods as a public defence solicitor and periods in a Procurator Fiscal's office may evolve over time. This might undermine the confidence which defendants have in public defence solicitors representing their interests vigorously. Goriely (1997: 3) points out that safeguarding independence is one of the problems of a public defence solicitor scheme as defenders develop close relationships with prosecutors.

Fixed fees

Fixed fees have been introduced for solicitors in Scotland providing legally aided representation under summary jurisdiction before Sheriff, Stipendiary Magistrate and District Courts[8]. The introduction of fixed fees changes the nature of the contract between the agent and the third-party payer (e.g. SLAB) from one of retrospective payment-for-service to a fixed fee regardless of service provided. The regulations set out fixed payments of two broad types for cases under summary jurisdiction:

1. **Core Payments** which will cover all work up to and including any diet at which a plea of guilty is made or accepted or plea in mitigation made together with the first 30 minutes of representation at a proof in mitigation or the first 30 minutes of any trial.
2. A series of **Additional Payments** for representation at trial or proof in mitigation beyond 30 minutes and representation at any deferred sentence diets.

It will still remain the case that legal aid will not be payable on an initial plea of guilty. Separate core and additional payments are proposed for cases marked by the procurator fiscal for hearing in the district court on the one hand and the Sheriff and Stipendiary Magistrate's Courts on the other. Counsel's fees are excluded from the fixed payments regime and the prescribed sums are net of VAT. Some outlays previously separately chargeable will be covered by the fixed payments.

In announcing the proposed scheme on 12th October 1998 the Minister of State for Home Affairs at the Scottish Office said that it was designed to bring about a saving of £10m in the cost of Summary Legal Aid. In 1997/98 (1996/97) payments (excl VAT) to solicitors for summary legal aid came to £40.1m (£40.7m)[10]. If a £10m reduction were achieved it would therefore represent a 25% reduction in payments to solicitors for summary legal aid work. Extrapolating from the pattern of cases in different categories in 1996/97 yields an estimate of the fees payable under the system as originally proposed by the Minister of the order of £30.2m. After representations from interested parties during a period of consultation the proposed regulations were modified by

---

[8] The changes are contained in the *Criminal Legal (Aid Fixed Payments) (Scotland) Regulations 1999* which took effect from April 1999 and which were subject to minor amendments by the *Criminal Legal Aid (Fixed Payments) (Scotland) Amendment Regulations 1999*.

[10] Scottish Legal Aid Board, Annual Report, 1996/97 and 1997/98.

raising both the core payments and some of the additional payments. The changes were such that based on the 1996/97 pattern of summary cases the savings were reduced from 25% to 21%.

Fixed fees have the advantage of reducing the cost of processing solicitors' bills for payment by the third-party payer. There would be no need to closely scrutinise every claim to calculate payment due if only one level of fee was permitted. There would also, probably, have to be some *ex post* auditing for 'quality' control unless some form of franchising scheme (such as that employed in England and Wales) were introduced under which solicitors had to pre-qualify to provide legal aid services. This would have its own set-up costs and its own need for auditing etc.

A number of commentators (Bowles, 1996; Gray, 1994; Gray, Fenn and Rickman, 1996; Dnes and Rickman, 1997) have pointed out that although the nature of the contract between the lawyer and the third-party payer changes with the move from fee-for-service to standard fee a principal-agent problem still remains, but it is a different one. The lawyer's incentives are reversed: under a fee-for-service contract the lawyer has an incentive to increase inputs even when they would not be cost effective (i.e. where the marginal cost of further work exceeds its marginal benefit) because his/her payment would rise; under fixed fees the incentives would be to provide the minimum level of inputs consistent with fulfilling the contract even where further inputs would be cost justified (i.e. where the marginal benefit of further work exceeds its marginal cost) because no increased payment would be received.

Rickman, Fenn and Gray (1999) summarise the results of their research on the introduction of standard (i.e. fixed) fees for criminal cases in England and Wales. They identify a number of ways in which solicitors might respond to the changes in incentives arising from the way in which standard fees operate in England and Wales. They present evidence that these have occurred. In particular they suggest that there appears to have been case-splitting. Multiple levels of fixed fees encourage solicitors to increase inputs in order to trigger a higher standard fee. Solicitors have changed their input mix increasing the use of inputs which are not covered by the standard fees.

The fundamental problem with the 'trigger levels' under the LAB's standard fee contract is that they are largely under the control of the supplier (agent). What is required is an objective indicator of when the extra effort which takes the fee beyond a trigger level is actually needed. It should be an indicator which is outwith the control of the supplier and should be an indicator of the complexity of the case (on the assumption that it is complexity that means extra effort is required from the supplier). The fixed fee scheme for Summary Legal Aid in Scotland appears to avoid this problem by having only one level of *Core Payment* with *Additional Payments* being related to trial length. Thus actions triggering additional payments are not wholly under the control of the accused person's agent and are subject to scrutiny by the court, e.g. number of charges, number of Crown witnesses *etc*. Nor does there appear to be any scope for case-splitting in the Scottish case because of the administrative mechanisms used to define the legally-aided case.

Proponents of fixed fees often argue that although the standard fee may represent under-remuneration of the lawyer when a case is complex or unusually long this will be balanced by cases where there would be over-remuneration when a case was very straightforward. In commenting on the proposals on 12th October 1998 Henry McLeish, then Minister of State for Home Affairs at the Scottish Office, said that there will be an element of such 'swings and roundabouts' under the Scottish fixed fee scheme. Notwithstanding the fact that such balancing is dependant on the choice of standard fee, this would only be true for those lawyers handling a large number of cases (Gray, 1994). Gray, Fenn and Rickman (1996) carried out a simulation of case-loads of different sizes based on a sample of legal aid payments in actual magistrates' court cases under fee-for- service contracts. They conclude that

> '... everything else being equal .... the introduction of a standard fee system is likely to have least effect on the overall payments to solicitors doing larger volumes of legal aid work ... solicitors doing small amounts of legal aid work would be much less likely to find that their overall payments remained equivalent to the earnings they would have received for the same cases under a fee-for service system. This is likely to discourage solicitors doing small amounts of legal aid work from participating that scheme'. (p.215)

This conclusion would appear to be borne out by an examination of the average payments for Summary Legal Aid to individual solicitors in Scotland in 1996/97. Chart 3 shows the average payments received by each solicitor against the number of cases paid. The chart plots the relationship between the average payment per case (excl. VAT) received by a solicitor for Summary Legal Aid on the vertical axis and the number of cases handled by that solicitor on the horizontal axis. The wide vertical dispersion of points to the left of the chart indicates that lawyers who do a small number of cases have wide variations in the *average* fee received per case. As the number of cases for each lawyer increases to the right along the horizontal axis the vertical variation is reduced. A horizontal line in the chart has been drawn at the average cost of all the cases in this data set. As can be seen lawyers with more than four hundred or so cases received an average payment per case close to the average payment over all cases. This is because with this number of cases the lawyer's case-load is representative of the total population of cases. At the other extreme the case-load of a lawyer with a small number of cases is unlikely to be representative of the total population of cases. This latter category of solicitors does not typically face 'swings and roundabouts'. Many of them only face 'swings' or only face 'roundabouts'.

The system inaugurated by the *Criminal Legal Aid Fixed Payments (Scotland) Regulations 1999* really comprise two changes to the pre-existing system. The first is the introduction of fixed fees. The second is the setting of the fixed fees at levels which will yield savings of around 22%. It is important to distinguish between the introduction of fixed fees and the effect of reducing overall expenditure on Summary Legal Aid.

Below simulations are carried out in an attempt to separate these two effects and to identify how they might impact on different categories of solicitors.

The simulations are carried out in two stages. In the first, the introduction of

REFORM OF LEGAL AID IN SCOTLAND

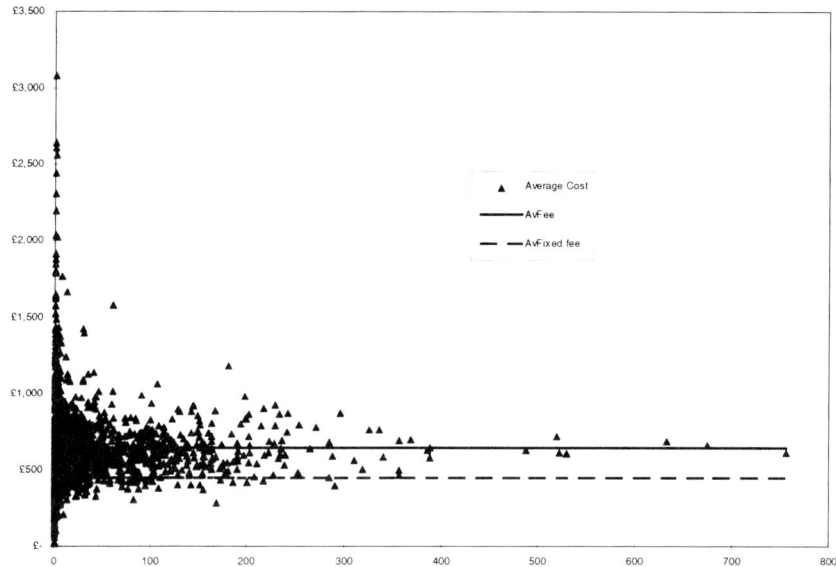

Chart 3. Solicitors' Average Fee for Summary Legal Aid by Number of Cases

a system of fixed fees which maintains expenditure on Summary Legal Aid at its 1996/97 level is simulated. This is referred to as a *fiscally neutral fixed fee*. Fiscal neutrality is maintained by setting the fixed fee at the average payment per case in 1996/97. In the second stage the effect of reducing the fixed fee to the level proposed in the regulations is simulated. This is referred to below as the *actual fixed fee*. The pre-existing payment system is referred to below as a 'fee-for-service contract'.

Assumptions

To carry out the simulations a number of assumptions must be made. These are:

1. The population of summary case-loads for which legal aid payments were made in 1996/97 (65,645 cases[11]) is representative of the composition of case-loads in a typical year.
2. Each solicitor's case-load is a random sample from a band of the case-load population.
3. Solicitors continue to provide the same level of input into summary legal aid cases and other cases after the introduction of fixed fees as they would

---
[11] This is the number of cases included in the data base of payments to solicitors supplied by the Scottish Office which compares with 67,085 cases shown in Appendix XII of the *Annual Report 1996/97, Scottish Legal Aid Board.*

have put into them under a fee-for-service contract. Thus it is assumed that no substitution takes place between legal aid work and other work as a consequence of the fixed fee.
4. In 1996/7 each solicitor generated a gross fee income net of VAT of £82,500 (£100,000 gross of VAT).
5. A time horizon of five years is used to examine the effects of the introduction of fixed fees.

The first assumption provides a basis for all of the calculations. The availability of data is really what dictates it. Were similar data available for a number of years it would be desirable to use that to arrive at some idea of representative case-loads. The second assumption is slightly stronger in that some defence agents may deal only with Sheriff Court cases rather than a mixture of District and Sheriff Court cases. Again it is the nature of the data which is available that forces us to make this assumption. The third assumption is the strongest. Economists will normally argue that when relative prices change suppliers will shift towards those areas where relative prices have risen. This would suggest a move away from summary Legal Aid towards other areas after the reduction in fees. Assumption three is made to allow the potential impact of the proposals on different solicitors' incomes to be assessed and thus to judge what sort of switch in activity might take place. The fourth assumption is necessary to give an indication of the relative impact of variations in Summary Legal Aid earnings on solicitors undertaking varying levels of legal aid work. The choice of level of gross fee income only effects the non-legal aid component of income and remains the same throughout the simulations. The choice of a five year horizon is somewhat arbitrary. However, it would be unwise to limit the horizon to just one year. Although the 'swings and roundabouts' analogy used by proponents of fixed fees does not apply to case-loads in any one year so that complex and simple cases do not necessarily net out, 'good' years may net out with 'bad' years over time.

The simulations proceed by drawing a random sample of case-loads of Summary Legal Aid for ten hypothetical solicitors in each of two case-load bands for each of five years. Assumption 3 gives the typical annual work load and total gross income for each solicitor. From assumption 2 the income from sources other than Summary Legal Aid in each year are obtained by deducting the income that was received for each case-load of Summary Legal Aid on a fee-for-service basis from £82,500. The income which would be earned from Summary Legal Aid with (i) a fiscally neutral fixed fee and (ii) the actual fixed fee are obtained by multiplying the number of cases in each simulated case-load by each fixed fee. The hypothetical Summary Legal Aid income generated in this way is then added to the other income obtained above to produce the simulated gross income for each solicitor in each of the five years.

The above simulation exercise is carried out for solicitors in two case-load bands: those with fewer than ten Summary Legal Aid cases per year[14]; and those with more than 40 but less than 50 cases[15].

---

[14] 50% of all solicitors in receipt of payment for Summary Legal Aid in 1996/97 undertook fewer than ten cases.

REFORM OF LEGAL AID IN SCOTLAND

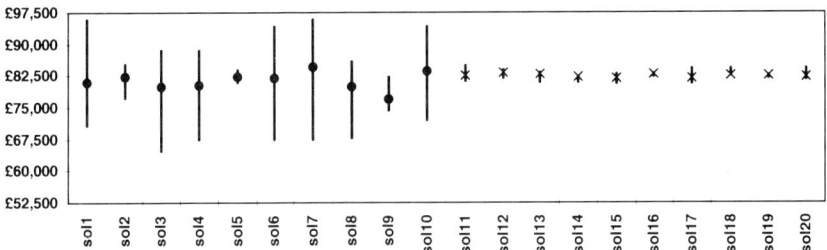

Chart 4. Variability of Gross Income with Fiscally Neutral Fixed Fee

Fiscally Neutral Fixed Fee

Chart 4 summarises the results for these two groups for the fiscally neutral fixed fee by showing the mean and the range between the maximum and minimum gross fee income of the ten hypothetical solicitors handling a Summary Legal Aid case-load of each of the two sizes for each of the five years. The solicitors 1 to 10 are hypothetical solicitors undertaking forty to forty-nine Summary Legal Aid cases per year. Those handling fewer than ten Summary Legal Aid cases are solicitors 11 to 20. The range between the maximum and minimum annual gross fee income over the five year period is indicated by the vertical line which runs from the minimum to the maximum.

The Chart shows that the gross incomes of the hypothetical solicitors handling fewer than ten cases (solicitors 11 to 20) are affected only slightly by the switch to a fixed fee. The mean gross income over the five years for each hypothetical solicitor is very close to their fee-for-service contract income of £82,500 as are the highest and lowest incomes of the ten solicitors. However, for the other group of solicitors (40 – 49 summary cases) the impact on gross fee income is to cause much greater variability for most (but not all) solicitors. Although the mean fee for these hypothetical solicitors in each year is relatively close to £82,500, the lowest falls to £64,000 in one year whilst the highest is around £95,000. The mean fees over the five years for each of the ten hypothetical solicitors range from just over £77,500 to around £84,500 with an overall average of £81,322. The most striking feature is that some solicitors face a range of almost £30,000 between their lowest and highest gross incomes over the five years. It is to be remembered that this effect has been produced by a fiscally-neutral fixed fee.

The preceding simulation suggests that if solicitors have a preference for a constant level of income it is more likely that those handling between forty and fifty summary legal aid cases would reconsider their involvement in legal aid than would those doing fewer than ten cases on the introduction of a fiscally neutral fixed fee.

---

[15] For these hypothetical solicitors summary legal aid income represented an annual average of between 31% and 42% of total annual income. They just make it into the top quartile of solicitors in terms of the number of summary legal aid cases per annum.

Actual Fixed Fee

The potential effects of the fixed fees introduced by the *Criminal Legal Aid Fixed Payments (Scotland) Regulations 1999* are now simulated. A weighted average of the core payments and additional payments for District Court cases and Stipendiary Magistrate and Sheriff Court cases has been calculated using the distribution of case types in 1996/97. On this basis the fixed fee used in the simulations reported below is £450. The underlying assumptions used in the simulations remain the same as in the earlier set of simulations. The Summary Legal Aid case loads are exactly the same as in the previous simulations and the gross fee income from sources other than Summary Legal Aid remain the same. All that changes is the value of the fixed fee used.

The results of these simulations are summarised in Chart 5. Again the mean and range between the maximum and minimum gross fee incomes of each group of ten hypothetical solicitors are shown for each of five years.

The average gross income in each year of the hypothetical solicitors undertaking fewer than ten cases falls by between £400 and £1,300 compared to the average fixed fee but are still very close to the base income of £82,500. The difference between the highest and lowest annual income for each hypothetical solicitor over the five years ranges from less than five hundred pounds to around three thousand seven hundred pounds. The averages for each solicitor across the five years range from just below £81,000 and £82,700. Thus the impact on gross fee income of the fixed fee for those solicitors undertaking fewer than ten cases is very small. The variation is also very small. It is therefore unlikely that those solicitors undertaking fewer than ten cases will change their behaviour.

The impact on the gross incomes of those solicitors handling between forty and fifty Summary Legal Aid cases is much greater. The average gross income in each year falls by around £8,000 as compared with the fiscally neutral fixed fee. The lowest gross fee income received by a firm in any year is down to £56,435 and the highest is down to £87,855. The mean fees over the five years for each of the ten hypothetical solicitors ranges from just under £69,000 to £76,655 with an average of £73,215. The range between the highest and lowest annual incomes of these firms over the five year period only changes slightly when compared with the fiscally neutral fixed fee but is large compared with the fee for service contract. The impact on the hypothetical solicitors

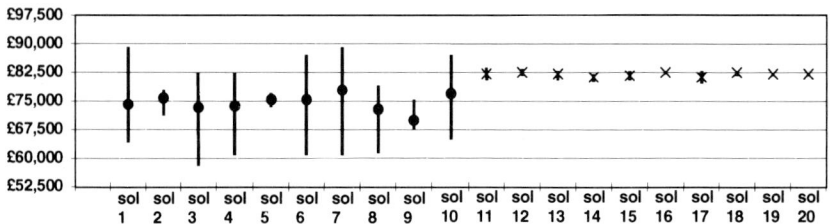

Chart 5. Variability of Gross Income with Actual Fixed Fee

undertaking forty to forty-nine Summary Legal Aid cases of a move from a fiscally neutral fixed fee to the proposed fixed fee is really the reduction in their mean fee over the period. This will further strengthen the need for these solicitors to reconsider the nature of their involvement in Summary Legal Aid.

The foregoing simulation suggest that of the two groups of hypothetical solicitors used in the simulations it is those undertaking more than forty but less than fifty cases whose gross fee income is affected most and who are more likely to alter their behaviour. The proposed fixed fee reduces their mean income over the five year period and increases its variability considerably. Neither the mean income nor variability of income is significantly affected for those hypothetical solicitors handling fewer than 10 Summary Legal Aid cases.

Comparisons

Above it was suggested that it would be useful to distinguish between the effects of a fiscally neutral fixed fee and the proposed fixed fee to identify the consequences of fixed fees *per se* and of the level of savings desired by the government. This is done in Chart 6 for the solicitors undertaking more than forty and less than fifty Summary Legal Aid cases. In addition to the fiscally neutral fixed fee and proposed fixed fee this chart also includes data for these hypothetical solicitors for a simulation in which fee-for-service is paid for summary Legal Aid but *at a rate 22% below that applying in 1996/97*[16]. Once again the vertical line shows the range between the highest and lowest annual income under each fee system for each hypothetical solicitor. Also shown is the mean gross fee income over the five years under each fee system for each hypothetical solicitor.

In the chart, for each solicitor reading from the left are shown: the situation with a fee-for-service contract at 22% below the fee level applying in 1996/97; a fiscally neutral fixed fee; and the actual fixed fee. A comparison of the second and third of these with the base gross fee income of £82,500 with no variation from year to year confirms that introducing a fiscally neutral fixed fee produces wide variation in fee income for most solicitors but with a mean fee income close to the base income. The shift to the actual fixed fee (from the fiscally neutral) has little further effect of variation but substantially reduces mean income for most firms.

The fee-for-service contract for Summary Legal Aid at 22% below 1996/97 levels produces considerably less variation in fee income from year to year than either fixed fee for all of the ten hypothetical solicitors. It yields lower mean income than the proposed fixed fee in only one case and then by only £500 out of more than £76,000. Thus in terms of impact on solicitors doing more than forty and less than fifty Summary Legal Aid cases a fee-for-service contract at a rate 22% below 1996/97 levels is to be preferred to the proposed fixed fee.

Chart 7 presents similar information for solicitors undertaking fewer than ten Summary Legal Aid cases. Again it can be seen that a switch from fee-for-

---

[16] This is done by simply reducing the income from Summary Legal Aid for each hypothetical solicitor in each year by 22%.

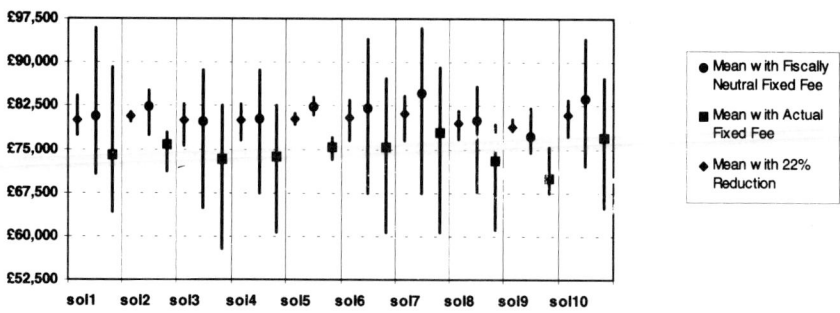

Chart 6. Variability of Gross Income (40–49 Cases)

service to a fiscally neutral fixed fee increases variability and a further switch to the actual fixed fee reduces the mean fee for each hypothetical solicitor. However for this group of hypothetical solicitors a fee-for-service contract at 22% below the 1996/97 fee is not necessarily an improvement on the actual fixed fee. Variability is reduced but in seven of the ten cases the mean fee under the proposed fixed fee is the higher. However, the mean fixed fee income is higher by only a few hundred pounds. This suggests that it would only require a mild preference for stability of income for these hypothetical solicitors to prefer the reduced fee-for-service contract.

Major Providers

The simulations reported above were carried out to ascertain the likely impact of the proposed fixed fee on solicitors who depend for *part* of their income on Summary Legal Aid cases. What is the likely impact for those solicitors who are almost solely dependent on this type of work? In 1996/97 there were seven solicitors who undertook more than 400 Summary Legal Aid cases in that year. Their gross income from this work ranged from £305,000 to £461,000. Their mean fee ranged from £608 to £717, a very narrow range compared to other groups of solicitors.

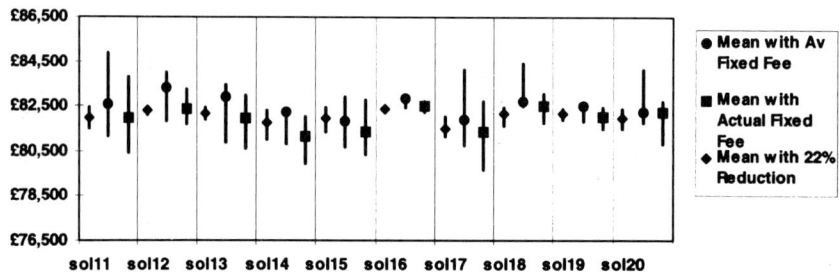

Chart 7. Variability of Gross Fee Income (Less than 10 Cases)

Table 6. Percentage Change in Gross Incomes of Largest Legal-Aid Providers

	Mixture of District and Sheriff	All Sheriff
Overall Reduction in Fees	−25%	−18.2%
Sol21	−23.4%	−17.0%
Sol22	−33.1%	−27.5%
Sol23	−21.5%	−15.0%
Sol24	−21.2%	−14.6%
Sol25	−30.2%	−24.4%
Sol26	−27.3%	−21.3%
Sol27	−21.4%	−14.8%

With this number of cases and mean fee close to the overall mean for summary cases their case loads appear to be fairly representative of the total population of cases in that year. Thus their case-load and gross fee income from Summary Legal Aid is unlikely to vary greatly from year to year. It is therefore not necessary to simulate the impact of fixed fees on these solicitors but simply to calculate the effect of the proposed fixed fee directly using their 1996/97 case loads. This is shown in Table 6.

The impact is calculated for two alternative assumptions relating to these solicitors' case-loads. The figure in the first column is arrived at by assuming that these seven firms each have a mixture of District and Sheriff Court summary cases similar to the overall population of solicitors. The reduction of gross fee income for these solicitors on this basis ranges from 21% to 33%. The figures in the second column are calculated on the assumption that the case-loads of these firms contain only Sheriff or Stipendiary Magistrates' Court cases. Here the reduction in gross fee income ranges from 14.6% to over 27.5%. The reduction in fees for Summary Sheriff Court cases implied by the new regulations is just over 18%. Under either assumption these solicitors face a very major reduction in annual gross fee income. Because this group of solicitors already has a fairly representative case-load, fixed fees will not increase the *variability* of their gross fee income only its *level*. For these solicitors the 'swings and roundabouts' analogy does apply in any one year.

Impact of Proposals

The introduction of a fixed fee *per se* (even at a level which would maintain expenditure on Summary Legal Aid at its existing level) affects different groups of solicitors differently. It will have little effect on the variability of overall gross fee income for infrequent providers. However, it will greatly increase the variability of gross fee income of those providers who do a significant amount of Summary Legal Aid work but who do not rely entirely on it. It is unlikely to affect the variability of gross fee income of the major providers of Summary Legal Aid.

The particular level of fixed fee introduced implies that as well as possible increased variability of gross fee income there is a significant lowering of the level of income for many solicitors. The effect on the overall gross fee income of infrequent providers of Summary Legal Aid will be small. On the other hand, those providers of a significant amount of Summary Legal Aid who do not rely on it wholly for their income will suffer an appreciable loss of income. The major providers whose income is heavily dependent on Summary Legal Aid will suffer a very significant reduction in gross fee income.

Reactions of Providers

The simulations reported above were carried out under the rather strong assumption that defence agents would not change their behaviour in response to the introduction of the proposed fixed fee. This was done to ascertain whether different groups of solicitors would be affected differently before going on to examine how they might then react. How they react depends on judgements on the relative weight given in the utility functions of solicitors to their own pecuniary interest and the interests of clients and the constraints placed upon them by professional standards of conduct and by the auditing and investigative powers of SLAB.

If solicitor behaviour with respect to a case is solely determined by the 'objective' requirements of their clients[18] then the simulations carried out above provide an accurate picture of what will happen to the incomes of solicitors. The infrequent providers may well continue to behave as before. Those who in the past handled a significant amount of Summary Legal Aid but were not wholly dependent on it are likely gradually to re-focus their work in areas other than Summary Legal Aid. Over time Summary Legal Aid will be carried out by specialist providers who have a large enough pool of cases to have a stable if lower gross fee income. They are also likely to introduce, where possible, more routine procedures to reduce the value of resources invested in Summary Legal Aid work.

On the other hand, if the dominant motivation of solicitors is their own financial well-being solicitors will reduce their professional input into cases until the resources committed are commensurate with the rewards available. This will allow them to spend more time on other more profitable work or to increase the number of summary cases they handle. Either way this would result in the interests of clients suffering.

These alternatives imply that the decreased 'risk' and level of public expenditure achieved by the proposed fixed fees is borne: in the first case, by legal practitioners; in the second, by accused persons.

---

[18] Implying that the work being done under the fee-for-service contract requires to be done to meet the professional standards set by the regulatory bodies.

References

Bevan, G. (1996). 'Has There been Supplier-Induced Demand for Legal Aid?'. *Civil Justice Quarterly*, Vol **15**, 98–114.

Bowles, R. (1996). 'Reform of Legal Aid and the Solicitors' Profession', in Stephen, F H (ed), *Access to Justice, Hume Papers on Public Policy*, **4** (4): 4–23.

Dnes, M. and Rickman, N. (1996). *Contracts for Legal Aid: an economic analysis of the UK government's proposals,* paper presented at the Maastricht Workshop in Law and Economics, (April), University of Limburg, Maastricht.

Goriely, T., Tata, C. and Paterson A. A. (1997). *Expenditure on Criminal Legal Aid: Report on a comparative pilot study of Scotland, England and Wales, and the Netherlands*, Central Research Unit, (August), The Scottish Office, Edinburgh, HMSO.

Goriely, T. (1997). Legal Aid Delivery Systems: Which offer the best value for money in mass casework? A summary of international experience'. (December), LCD Research Series.

Gray, A., Fenn, P. and Rickman, N. (1996). 'Controlling Lawyers' Costs through Standard Fees: An Economic Analysis' in Young, D and Wall, D (eds), *Access to Criminal Justice*, London : Backstone Press.

Houlden and Balking (1985). 'Quality and Cost Comparisons of Private Bar Indigent Defense systems: Contract vs. Ordered Assigned Counsel', *Journal of Criminal Law and Criminology*, **79**: 176.

Lord Chancellor's Department (1995). *Legal Aid – Targeting Need*, Cm 2854, HMSO, London, November.

Lord Chancellor's Department (1997a). *Striking the Balance*, CM 3305, June, HMSO, London..

Lord Chancellor's Department (1997b). *Future of Legal Aid and the Civil Justice System*, October, Lord Chancellor's Department.

Lord Chancellor's Department (1998a). *Access to Justice with Conditional Fees*, October, Lord Chancellor's Department.

Manson-Smith, D. (1995) . *The Legal System of Scotland*, Scottish Consumer Council, HMSO, Edinburgh.

Samuel, E. (1996). 'Criminal Legal Aid Expenditure: Supplier or System Driven: The Case of Scotland', in Young D. and Wall D. (eds), *Access to Criminal Justice,* London. : Blackstone Press.

Scottish Legal Aid Board, *Annual Report*, various years, Edinburgh.

Scottish Office (1998). *Criminal Legal Aid Fixed Payments* (Scotland) Regulations.

Spangenberg, R. (1990). *Statement before the Subcommittee On Administrative Law and Government Relations*, US House of Representatives, regarding the re-authorisation of the Legal Services Corporation, May 9, Washington, DC.

Stephen, F. H. (1998). *Legal Aid Expenditure in Scotland: Growth, Causes and Alternatives*, Law Society of Scotland, Edinburgh.

Cost Shifting and Pre-trial Settlement

Brian G M Main and Andrew Park[1]

Introduction

The procedural rules of civil law in any society have an impact with far-reaching consequences. These rules affect not only those disputes that arrive before a judge or jury, but also those which enter the legal system and settle before trial (and settlement is the outcome in over 90% of all civil cases entering the legal system). Indeed, they also affect the conduct and resolution of disputes that do not even get as far as the legal system. This is because all parties to such disputes are able to anticipate what is likely to happen if they do arrive before a judge or jury, and this anticipation is factored into the way in which the parties negotiate any settlement of the dispute in hand. This last effect is often referred to as 'negotiating in the shadow of the law'.

One particularly clear aspect of civil court procedure that looms large in such considerations is the way in which the costs of legal proceedings are allocated between the disputing parties. The clearest contrast is between the so-called American rule, whereby both sides pay their own costs irrespective of the outcome, and the so-called English rule (actually prevalent almost everywhere except in North America), whereby the losing party is responsible for 'all' the costs of both sides. In reality the losing party is only responsible for those of the winning side's costs that the court decides are reasonable, but this still creates a marked difference between the two rules.

Furthermore, as anyone entering the legal system quickly realises, there are other nuances involved in making pre-trial offers. A long-standing arrangement, broadly known as 'payments into court', allows defendants to make, without prejudice to any denial of liability, an offer to settle. If, on losing the case, the offer turns out to have been more generous than the amount finally awarded by the judge or jury[2], then the defendant is relieved of all costs (own and those of the other side) from the time that the offer was made. Under recent reforms introduced to the English High Court and inspired by the Report of

---

[1] Thanks are due to two referees for their invaluable comments and suggestions.

[2] The existence of any offer is only made known to the judge at the end of the trial when the costs are being apportioned, i.e., after the verdict has been delivered.

Lord Woolf (1996), this ability to make formal pre-trial settlement offers has been extended to the claimant (as 'Rule 36' offers). Here, if the claimant has made an offer to settle that is less than the judge subsequently awards then, in addition to having the losing defendant pay their costs, the claimant also enjoys an uplift of some 10 percentage points in the rate of interest used to compute the level of damages due (from the time of the incident that gave rise to the claim), with the penal rate of interest starting from the time at which the claimant made the relevant offer to settle.

These various institutional arrangements are designed to encourage pre-trial settlement and, hence, reduce the very obvious costs (both emotional and financial) of going through a trial procedure. But much of the theory in this area leads to rather ambiguous conclusions as to the efficacy of such procedures. There is also a marked shortage of empirical evidence relating to pre-trial settlements, as most of such agreements are bound by confidentiality restrictions. To circumvent these data problems, the research described below uses the approach of experimental economics to examine the various distinct civil court procedural arrangements that are aimed at improving access to justice through lowering the expected costs of disputants by enhancing their chances of reaching a pre-trial settlement. We do this in a laboratory setting in which participants assume the role of plaintiff (or 'claimant' in the English modern usage, or 'pursuer' in the Scottish system) or defendant ('defender' in Scotland). For the sake of uniformity, the recently revised English legal terms of 'claimant' and 'defendant' will be used hereafter.

To focus on the impact of the various cost-shifting rules in force in the course of an experiment, it is arranged that participants do not know against whom they are negotiating (by use of a computer network to organise and co-ordinate the rounds of negotiation). Individuals assume the same role throughout each two-hour laboratory session and up to 12 'cases' are simulated in each session with the position in terms of expected damages, probability of winning and expected costs if it ends in trial, all laid out in advance. More details of the exact experimental procedures followed are given below.

The general findings of this research project suggest that the various procedural arrangements that affect how legal costs are divided between the parties of disputes that end up in court do not make any significant measurable difference on the propensity of these cases to reach a pre-trial settlement. These arguments do, however, affect bargaining power to the extent that the level of settlement agreed by the parties is significantly influenced by the type of cost-shifting rule in place. Based on this evidence, recent procedural changes introduced after the Lord Woolf inspired changes in the English High Court are, therefore, likely to enhance the negotiating power and improve the outcomes for claimants but unlikely to impact on the proportion of cases reaching pre-trial settlement. Analysis of the dynamics of negotiating behaviour also reveals some interesting patterns that may be of interest to practitioners in this area.

In the next section of the paper, some feeling is given for the importance of the various cost-shifting rules by reference to a few well known cases in which they played a significant part. The general theory surrounding the analysis of negotiating behaviour in such circumstances is then explained. This is followed by a section in which the experimental procedures are described and a review of the results obtained is presented. The paper ends with a general summary of the findings and a discussion of the policy implications.

The analysis of how cost-shifting rules work

A powerful example of the working of defendant offers (or payments into court) is provided by the case[3] of Kwasi Minta, a person badly burned in the Kings Cross Tube Station fire in 1987. Having turned down a payment into court of £355,000 from London Regional Transport (LRT), he was awarded £110,427 damages in March 1997 after an eight day hearing in the High Court. Because he had turned down an offer from LRT that was more generous than that subsequently awarded by the judge at trial, Mr Minta was liable for much of LRT's legal expenses since the date that their offer was so rejected. This left Mr Minta liable for some £150,000 of LRT's legal expenses as well as his own expenses from that date. This was clearly a very negative outcome for Mr Minta.

In a case involving someone rather better known that Mr Minta, William Roache (who plays Ken Barlow in Coronation Street) instigated a libel suit against the Sun[4] and, in the course of this, he rejected a payment into court of £50,000 – only to see the jury subsequently award him exactly £50,000 in damages. Because Mr Roache had failed to 'beat the offer' (that was figuratively on the table), he was left liable for much of the Sun's legal expenses since the date of the rejected offer, as well as his own expenses since that date – even though he 'won' the case. Mr Roache subsequently sued his solicitors for poor advice, but lost this case and ended up with a legal bill said[5] to be in the region of £200,000.

A third, and final example, is provided by the ex-prime minister of the Republic of Ireland, Mr Albert Reynolds who sued the Times for defamation after they had suggested that he lied to the Diall. After a long trial, Mr Reynolds won his case but was awarded zero monetary damages by the jury. The judge in the case subsequently revised this award upward to the sum of one penny (£0.01). This was, unfortunately for Mr Reynolds, rather less than the £5,005 already offered as a payment into court by the newspaper. The consequent legal bill faced by Mr Reynolds (technically the victor in this case, but caught on the wrong side of a payment into court) was said to have been in the region of £1million.

The general framework in which these pre-trial negotiations take place is most easily illustrated in terms of a numerical example. For the sake of continuity we will utilise numbers that are actually used in the experiments to be discussed below. Let us assume, on the basis of the evidence to hand (and assuming this evidence is clear to both sides), the probability a judge will find

---

[3] Reported in the Times on 27 March 1997.
[4] Reported in the Scotsman on 10 March 1998.
[5] The Times July 10, 1998.

Table 1. The parameters used

Parameter	Value
Probability of claimant victory, P	0.75
Level of total legal costs, C	£6,000
Maximum damages, Y_{max}	£10,000
Minimum damages, Y_{min}	£2,000

for the claimant is 0.75 (and there is, therefore, a 25% chance that the claim will be dismissed at trial). Assume, further, that if liability is successfully proved then the range of damages likely to be awarded will be between £2,000 and £10,000 with each value in that range being equally likely. Finally, let the legal costs arising from trial be £3,000 to each side (and therefore £6,000 in total). These parameters are shown in Table 1.

In terms of these numbers, it can be seen that under the English rule with no additional complications the claimant has an expected gain at trial of £3000 (which is a 75% chance of gaining an average of £6000 in damages net of a 25% chance of gaining no damages and having to pay the costs of both sides, £6000). The defendant, on the other hand, faces an expected costs at trial of £9000 (which is a 25% chance of having to pay out nothing if the case is dismissed and a 75% chance of having to pay out the total £6000 legal costs of both sides on top of the average £6000 damages if liability is found proved). The existence of legal costs provides both sides with an incentive to reach an out-of-court settlement[6]. In the parlance of negotiation there is £6000 'on the table' available for the mutual gain of both sides. The question that remains is, of course, who gets what part of it? That is, should the pre-trial settlement be down near the £3000 mark, hence giving the bulk of the gains to the defendant, or should the agreement be up around the £9000 mark, giving most of the advantage to the claimant?

Of course, if the litigants have differing views with regard to their respective prospects at trial, then there may be even greater perceived gains from reaching a pre-trial settlement. The following figure helps illustrate the situation for the case of two litigants who are relatively pessimistic, in the sense that the defendant expect the claimant to do better at trial than the claimant herself or himself expects to do. In this case, the expected trial outcome before costs for the defendant, O_d, is greater than the expected trial outcome before costs for the claimant, O_c. Add the implications of a loser-pays legal costs regime and

---

[6] This approach draws on the model of Landes (1971), Posner (1973) and Gould (1973). In this model the litigants can have differing views of the likely outcome at trial. If they are relatively pessimistic (i.e., the claimant expects less chance of winning or lower damages at trial than the defendant) then the prospect of legal costs enlarges the already positive money on the table. If, on the other hand, the litigants are relatively optimistic there will be no pre-trial settlement that leaves them better off than they expect to be at trial (as the claimant expects to gain a lot and the defendant expects to pay much less, if anything). Even here, however, the prospect of legal costs draws the parties together and may, if large enough, be sufficient to induce the parties to agree to a pre-trial settlement.

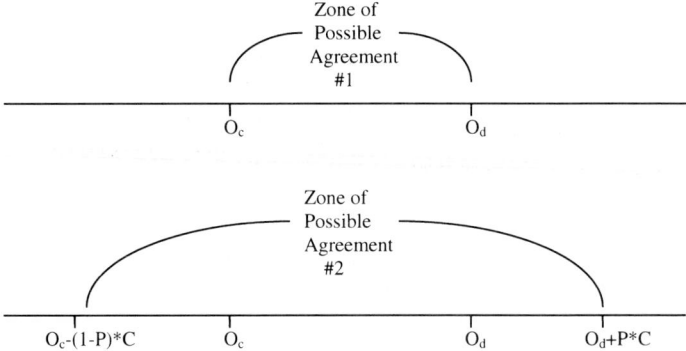

Key:

C_d	costs of going to trial incurred by the defendant
C_c	costs of going to trial incurred by the claimant
$C = C_d + C_c$	total legal costs
O_d	expected trial outcome, before costs, as seen by defendant
O_c	expected trial outcome, before costs, as seen by claimant

Figure 1. The Impact of Legal Costs

the money on the table (or, zone of possible agreement) increases further. From the figures and analysis below, it can be seen that the presence of legal costs enhances the mutual gain available by reaching a pre-trial settlement.

Many jurisdictions modify their usual cost-shifting rule in an attempt to concentrate the minds of the litigants and to encourage an early out-of-court settlement. The most common procedural arrangement of this type is the defendant's offer to settle, whereby if a defendant makes a genuine offer to settle which is refused and, if the judge subsequently awards at trial a quantum of damages that is less than this offer, then all of the legal costs after the point at which the defendant's offer was refused fall on the claimant, even though the claimant is the 'successful' party. The logic here is consistent with the logic of the 'loser pays' rule, namely that the intransigent party should be held responsible for all costs of resolving a dispute. In simple cases under the unadorned English rule, the intransigent party is the party who either refused to recognise a genuine claim (defined as genuine by the judge's ruling – the unsuccessful defendant) or who prosecuted an unreasonable claim (defined as unreasonable by the judge's ruling – the unsuccessful claimant).

With the defendant offer, this logic of intransigence extends to the claimant who refuses what the judge, by the very award of a certain quantum of damages, defines to have been a perfectly reasonable offer. Such a claimant must, therefore, be deemed intransigent from the moment the reasonable offer was refused and, hence, must bear the consequences in terms of related legal costs incurred since that date. The way this mechanism (defendant offers) is meant to work is that it should encourage the defendant to make 'generous' offers to settle by making it 'cheap' to do so. It is cheap because by this mechanism the prospect of having to bear the legal costs of both sides can be avoided or at least reduced. It also makes it expensive for the claimant to refuse an offer, as this might lead the claimant to being liable for the legal costs of both sides. As legal costs rise precipitously once a case reaches the courtroom, these mechanisms are potentially very powerful as they generally come into play during the period of case preparation before the trial stage is reached.

The use of offers into court, whereby the empirical outcome of the trial process is made conditional on the pre-trial settlement offers of one or both parties, is now commonplace in many jurisdictions. The arrangement is generally referred to as either payments into court or Calderbank offers in England and Wales (Woolf, 1995, p. 194), as judicial offers or tenders[7] in Scotland (Macphail, 1988, p. 471), and as 'lodgement in satisfaction' in the Republic of Ireland. In the USA, Rule 68 in the federal courts (Cooper, 1996) and many state-wide variants (e.g., Michigan Rule of Court, Rule 2.405, or California Rule 998) move the cost-shifting regime in the direction of loser pays (the English rule) and away from each party paying their own costs[8].

The logic of these procedural rules is similar to that often given to justify the basic loser-pays English rule of allocating costs. Under the hypothesis that the trial outcome represents the 'truth' (or as near as we are likely to get to it), then the party ruled to be in the wrong in a civil trial[9] is held to be the intransigent party and the one who should bear the costs of the trial process. Under defendant offers into court, this logic is extended further to the situation where, even if held to be liable, the defendant is relieved of all responsibility for costs[10] from the point where the defence makes a good faith offer to settle that is in excess of what the judge subsequently awards. Here the claimant, by rejecting such an offer, is implicitly deemed to be intransigent.

In jurisdictions such as Australia and Canada[11] systems were introduced in the 1980s allowing the claimant to make similar offers to settle. In 1991 these systems[12] came to the attention of Lord President Hope who had his private office conduct some research into these matters. Lord Hope also drew the existence of these Australian and Canadian rules to the attention of Lord Woolf's Committee of inquiry. Lord Woolf (1996, p112) regarded offers to settle as

---

[7] One legal authority, Walker (1974, p. 1099), refers to cases as far back as 1847 in his discussion of tenders in Scotland.

[8] See Rowe and Anderson (1996, p. 143).

[9] That is either a defendant against whom a claim is upheld or a claimant whose claim is thrown out.

[10] The extent of relief from costs, whether including lawyer's fees and expert witness fees etc. in addition to court fees, varies from jurisdiction to jurisdiction.

[11] See Hutchinson (1985) and Civil Justice Quarterly (1986).

[12] Discussed at Chapter 34A in the Rules of the Court of Session. The rules in question existed in British Columbia, New Brunswick, Nova Scotia, Ontario and Saskatchewan in Canada and in New South Wales, Queensland, South Australia and Victoria in Australia.

'capable of making an important contribution to the change of culture which is fundamental to the reform of civil justice' and included among his recommendations a system of offers to settle. This system would allow the claimant to make an offer to settle, and to enjoy additional interest[13] on any damages awarded in the event of beating this offer (i.e., where the offer is not accepted and the award at trial is for at least as much as the amount at which the claimant offered to settle).

In Scotland, the similar idea of "pursuer's offers" received a favourable comment from the Cullen Report (1995: p59), which backed the proposals then under consideration by the Court of Session Rules Council noting that "the defender should normally be found liable in expenses at an increased level where the pursuer, i.e., claimant, has succeeded in 'beating his own offer' ". Indeed, after some consultation, the Rules Council of the Court of Session agreed to introduce a system of pursuer's offers (i.e., claimant's offers to settle) for an experimental period of two years. The innovation was not universally popular and, as explained below, the actual wording and design of the rule was unfortunate, the penalty chosen being "not the most appropriate", in the words of the Court of Session Rule Book.

Instituted with effect from 23 September 1996, the new procedure was withdrawn some seven weeks later, on 14 November 1996. The original Act of Sederunt[14] included the following terms in Rule 34A.6(2)b,

> Where the pursuer is awarded a sum equal to or more than the sum specified in the offer to settle, he shall be entitled, from the defender to whom the offer to settle was made –
> a) unless the court otherwise orders, to the expenses of process (including any additional fee under Rule 42.14) as taxed by the Auditor; and
> b) to a sum equal to the taxed amount of those expenses (excluding any additional fee under Rule 42.14).

Not only was this procedure precipitately withdrawn, but an award that qualified under its terms was denied after appeal to the Inner House of the Court of Session[15]. The design of this cost-shifting rule can be seen to be flawed in two ways. First, as the sanction in section b) above is calculated on taxed expenses and as the offer could be submitted any time before judgement is made (or

---

[13] In the final (1996) Report, Lord Woolf suggests: a 25 percentage point interest premium on damages of up to £10,000; a premium of 15 percentage points on damages of more than £10,000 and up to £50,000; and a premium of 5 percentage points on awards over £50,000. These interest payments are to run from the date of the relevant offer to settle. When actually implemented in April 1999, the interest rate penalty has a more modest ten percentage points ceiling.

[14] The devolved power under which such procedural changes are made in the Scottish legal system. Rules of the Court of Session Amendment No. 6, 1996 (S.I. 1996 No. 2769).

[15] The case in question is William Copland Taylor against Marshall's Food Group and was heard by the Lord President (Lord Rodger of Earlsferry), Lord Coulsfield and Lord Allanbridge. Opinion 26 June 1998 (*Scottish Legal Times* 1998, 1022).

before the jury retires to consider its judgement) there is, far from an incentive to settle early, an incentive to delay serious negotiation. With delay comes increased costs to both sides and, hence, the prospect of additional gains to the claimant should the conditions of clause 34A6(2)b be applied. Concerns were also raised regarding cases where the quantum of damages is not in dispute. In such cases it was claimed that the claimant could obtain an advantage by making an offer to settle at that level, thereby increasing the stakes for the defendant. In such cases, of course, the defendant has a not dissimilar advantage through the use of a payment into court (or judicial offer or tender as it is variously known in Scotland).

Second, there is serious legal debate on whether the authority exists to award anything more than actual expenses incurred, and specifically to award a penalty beyond the actual expenses incurred in preparation of the case for trial. It is on this second consideration that the legal arguments centred at the appeal stage, but from an economic perspective it is the first that is the more important. It is clear that careful modelling of the incentive effects of any such procedural rule is vital.

In England and Wales, however, there has been an introduction of claimant offers to settle in the High Court under the new procedural rules introduced in April 1999, and specifically under Part 36 of these rules. This allows the claimant to make an offer to settle which, if subsequently declined and beaten at trial, entitles the claimant to a premium or uplift on the interest rate charged to compute damages owed of up to 10 percentage points over and above the base rate from the date on which the offer was refused (or 21 days after an offer being made in the case of no response). In such cases the claimant is already, of course, entitled to reimbursement of legal costs from the defendant, but under such circumstances indemnity costs (a somewhat more generous interpretation of what qualifies for reimbursement) may apply.

Landes (1971), Posner (1973) and Gould (1973) develop the analysis introduced above in Figure 1 to suggest the range in which settlements should take place. They also put forward the view that any procedural arrangements (such as offers to settle) that enhance the settlement range will consequently increase the likelihood of the parties reaching a pre-trial settlement. Chung (1996) and some of our own work[16] extends this line of approach. When one party has access to relevant information unknown to the other party, a slightly different approach is needed as can be found in the work of Bebchuk (1984), Reinganum and Wilde (1986) and, again, some of our own recent work. But the experiments and analysis described in the remainder of this paper deal solely with situations where both parties have access to the same information.

Extending the simple analysis offered in Figure 1 above to accommodate judicial offers to settle can be accomplished by developing the analysis of Chung (1996). Figure 2 illustrates the situation for defendant offers (or payments into court). The claimant's prospects at trial are reduced if they refuse a judicial offer to settle from the defendant. And the more generous the offer

---

[16] See the papers by Main and Park reviewed in Appendix B at the end of this paper.

made by the defendant, the lower the expected gains at trial for the claimant. The defendant, of course, does not wish to make too generous an offer or it will be readily accepted. Thus, to take an extreme example, if the defendant made a payment into court of £10000 (the maximum damages possible) and the claimant was foolish enough to reject it, then at trial the expected outcome for the claimant would be an unattractive loss of £1500 (which comprises a 75% chance of winning £6000 damages on average, but having to pay all of the £6000 costs, owing to the defendant's offer being always at least as good as any award the judge might make, and a 25% chance of losing the case altogether and again having to pay all of the costs). From the defendant's perspective, the expected outcome at trial is now a loss of £4500 (which comprises a 75% chance of having to pay damages of £6000 on average when the claimant wins their case, but no prospect of having to pay any legal costs, no matter what the liability decision).

In fact, at the upper end of the offer range, the defendant need never offer more than £6480 by way of settlement as with such a payment into court the maximum expected loss at trial is exactly £6480. Offers to settle above that level would be more expensive than going to trial and so will not be made. This also has an impact a the power end of the offer spectrum. Whereas before an offer of £3000 would leave the defendant no better off than the expectation of going to trial, now an offer as low as £2640 leaves the claimant no better off than going to trial. This reduction is because with an offer of £2640 on the table there is a finite (albeit small, probability that the judge's award would be less than £2640 and hence leave the claimant facing the prospect of having to pay the total legal bill of both sides (£6000) even if they 'win' in court.

The general point here is that when the defendant is free to make offers to settle through payments into court the claimant suffers a penalty (in having to pay the total trial costs even when successful) if the trial judgement is less generous than this offer. In such circumstances, therefore, the claimant must make the final demand from the defendant in the light of any 'offer into court' already made by the defendant. This adds a stage to the analysis whereby the defendant must calculate what offer into court is optimal. The impact on the defendant is to increase the bargaining strength by shifting the zone of possible agreement towards lower settlements.

In such a situations, therefore, we expect the agreed settlements to be in this restricted range of £2640 to £6480. Note that this is markedly in the defendant's interest. Note also that the bargaining range has reduced form the £3000 to £9000 range that applied when only the unadorned English rule applied. From a Landes-Posner-Gould perspective, this reduced range might suggest a lower chance of the parties reaching an out-of-court settlement and, therefore, a higher proportion of disputes ending up at trial.

When this analysis is extended to allowing the claimant to make offers to settle the situation becomes more complex and is not described in detail here. But the logic is similar to that for defendant offers. In the experiments that we conduct, we represent the working of the claimant offers to settle rule (Rule 36 Offers in the High Court) by increasing the awarded damages by half (+50%) for those cases where the dispute ends up at trial and the judge awards a

COST SHIFTING AND PRE-TRIAL SETTLEMENT

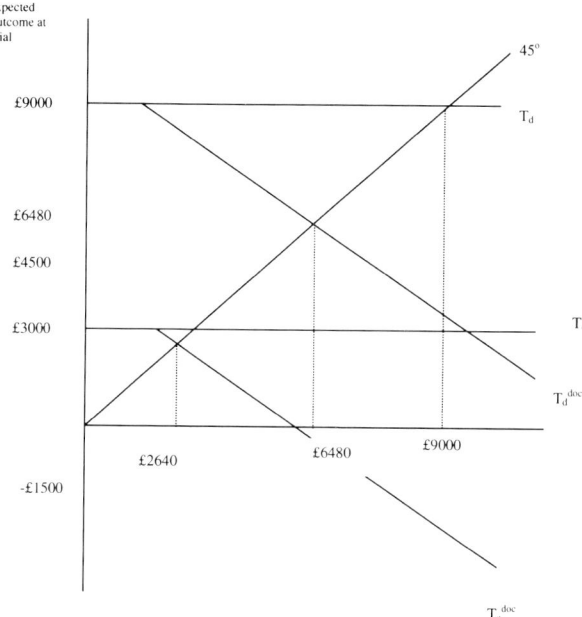

Figure 2. Settlement range under English rule with defendant offers into court

quantum for the claimant that is more than the amount at which the claimant had offered to settle. In most cases the effect of this will be more dramatic than the 10% penal interest rate incorporated in the recent High Court procedural innovations, but the 50% rule is straight forward and easy for the experimental subjects to understand. With the added complication of claimant offers to settle on top of defendant offers to settle, the likely settlement range moves to £3911 to £7202. These predictions are summarised for the three combinations of rules in Table 2.

Thus, it is predicted that the settlement rate will decline in turn with the introduction of each of the cost-shifting rules as the settlement range or Zone of Possible Agreement (Zopa) falls in magnitude. The 'best-guess' predictions for the level of settlement are the mid-points of each of the bargaining ranges

Table 2. Predictions of the theory

	No cost shifting	Defendant cost-shifting	Two-way cost-shifting
Settlement range	6000	3840	3291
Minimum	3000	2640	3911
Mid-Point	6000	4560	5557
Maximum	9000	6480	7202

shown in Table 2. Thus, it is expected that the level of settlement value will fall with the move from the English rule alone (£6000) to defendant payments into court (£4560) and will rise again with the move to two-way offers to settle (£5557).

Details of the experiments

Method

The participants of the experiments have the trial process made intuitive by simulating its outcome through the use of a roulette wheel to determine liability. For those cases in which the court recognises a valid claim, the level of damages is determined by drawing a numbered ball from a tombola cage. In each case the exact numbers and proportions involved are carefully explained to participants. Hence, the 75% probability that the claimant will win at trial is explained by having the numbers 1 through 9 on the spin of the roulette wheel signify that the case is thrown out at trial and the numbers 10 through 36 indicating that the claimant's case is successful. If a zero appears the wheel is re-spun. In those cases where the roulette wheel shows a number 10 through 36 (i.e., the claimant is successful at trial) the quantum of damages awarded by the judge is simulated by then spinning a tombola cage containing numbered balls with one ball for each number 20 through 100. The first ball drawn at random then represents the size of the damages awarded by the judge as measured in £100s. Thus, the numbered ball 69 would indicate a damages award of £6900.

In addition, the participants are provided with documentation laying out the basis of the claim, the chances of the claimant winning and the range and probability of damages that would be awarded in the outcome of liability being proved. Participants (who assume the role of a claimant or a defendant throughout the typically two-hour laboratory session) are also made familiar with the computer software that allows them to exchange demands and offers with the other randomly assigned and anonymous party. Some practice runs are allowed before measurement begins to ensure that all participants are made comfortable with the technology and know how things work.

Participants are also made aware of the way in which they will be paid for their participation. This involves a basic £5 fee for turning up and then a payment determined by each individual's performance in the negotiations. The reward structure essentially makes each £1000 they are negotiating worth £1.00 to them in real take-home money. To prevent initial success or failure in the early games conditioning play in later games the whole of this reward is determined by a single game but the identity of which game is the 'important one' is not revealed until the end of the session when it is drawn at random from the games played. In one game[17], for example, defendants start off each game with a notional £21000 (i.e. £21) and claimants start off each game with a notional £6000 (i.e. £6). If they successfully reach a pre-trial settlement the claimant-

---

[17] This refers to the two-way offers games.

defendant pair or dyad have, therefore, £27 to share between them, but if they end up at trial there will be only £26 shared between them – in additional to their guaranteed appearance fees. Fees are doubled for the professional participants.

The institutional cost-shifting rule (who bears what part of the total costs if the case ends up at trial) is varied once in each session. As explained above, participants are encouraged to take the negotiation seriously by having their payment made dependent on their performance in these sessions. The existence of legal costs makes it in the interest of both parties to settle out of court, but there is a tension as one side wishes to settle high and the other low. Offers and counter-offers are exchanged between parties over a computer network using appropriate user-friendly software.

When offers into court are introduced, the defendant (for defendant offers) or both parties (for two-way offers) can make offers into court. As explained above, these have a potentially important influence on who pays what part of the costs should the case end up at trial. The only 'costs' involved in making such a formal offer is that the party making the offer is not subsequently allowed to make a less generous offer. Thus, a defendant making a £5000 payment into court (defendant offer) would not in a later round of negotiation within the same game be able to reduce their offer to £4500. Similarly if a claimant makes a £6000 formal offer to settle then they cannot subsequently increase their demand to £6500 while still negotiating the same case. More than one formal payment into court or offer to settle can be made, but these have to be more generous to the other side than the pre-existing one.

If the parties refrain from using the formal 'offer to settle' mechanisms when available then they are free to increase or decrease their offers and demands in each round of negotiation during each 3-minute game. The price of such flexibility is that this type of bid and counter-bid are totally informal and have no influence on who subsequently bears the legal costs if the case ends up a trial. Only where a bid is designated via the software and made clear to both sides as an offer into court do any possible cost implications arise. Each game is time-limited to three minutes and those bargaining pairs who have yet to reach a pre-trial settlement at the end of three minutes are automatically sent to trial where the combination of the roulette wheel and the tombola cage, as described above, simulates a judge's decision. Although participants maintain the same role throughout (claimant or defendant), they play in anonymous and randomly matched pairs in each and every game of the two-hour session.

Two aspects are studied: (i) the proportion of cases that settle without going to trial under each of the various cost-shifting arrangements, and (ii) the level of settlement agreed in those cases settling out of court. A series of five experiments is reported on here. These involve three types of cost-rule repeated on two groups of participants. The three types of cost rule are (i) English rule; (ii) English rule with defendant offers into court; and (iii) English rule with both sides able to make offers into court (two-way offers). Each of these is studied, first using groups of undergraduate student volunteers as participants and, second, using three groups of professional participants who more closely approximate the types of individuals actually involved on a daily basis in negotiating under these various procedural rules. The three groups of professionals used are (i) practising solicitors; (ii) post-graduate students in the final stages of their 'Diploma in Legal Practice'; and (iii) MBA students, all of whom have at least three years of post-graduate work experience.

There is certainly substantial novelty in the context of the application but these experiments followed fairly standard protocols and well developed procedures documented in Davies and Holt (1993), Friedman and Sunder (1994), Hey (1991), and Kagel and Roth (1995). One previous attempt to utilise experimental methods in this area can be found in the work of Coursey and Stanley (1988), although their experimental design more closely resembles what is known as the 'split the dollar' problem whereby there is a pot of money 'on the table' and the parties are trying to agree who will get what share of it, although neither party currently owns it. This fails to reflect the key aspect of pre-trial negotiation, namely that one party currently owns resources and that the other is trying to claim part of these resources. This can be expected to lead to a very different frame of reference to the negotiation. Our experimental design allows for this important effect.

Results

Settlement propensity and level

An overview of the results obtained for the first experiments that relied on undergraduates is provided in Table 3 below. The situation with the undergraduate students is somewhat complicated as a number of separate experiments were undertaken comparing pairs of cost rules, but the net result was 114 games of the English rule alone, 222 games of defendant payments into court, and 108 games of two-way offers to settle. In Table 3, it can be seen that the proportion of cases in which pre-trial settlement occurs is unaffected by the nature of the cost-shifting rule (72.8% settle with the English rule alone, 73.9% settle with the addition of defendant offers, and 71.3% settle with two-way offers, i.e., both the defendant and the claimant able to make offers into court). Unsurprisingly, these numbers are not significantly different from each other in a statistical sense.

Table 3. Impact of varying cost rules (Undergraduate students)

	English rule alone	Defendant offers	Two-way offers
Settlements (%)	83 (72.8%)	164 (73.9%)	77 (71.3%)
Trial (%)	31 (28.2%)	58 (26.1%)	31 (28.4%)
No. of games	114	222	108
Average Settlement (£)	6627	6475	6599
Standard Deviation	826	793	1227
Max. (£)	8500	14900	13000
Min. (£)	3500	4000	4000

COST SHIFTING AND PRE-TRIAL SETTLEMENT   55

In terms of the level of settlement, the impact of variation in cost-shifting rules is consistent with the predictions of theory. The results presented in Table 3 show that with the addition of defendant offers the average level of settlement moves from £6627 to £6457 – a statistically significant move in the favour of the defendant, reflecting the bargaining advantage gained by the defendant being able to make payments into court, i.e. defendant offers to settle. Then when the ability to make offers into court is also extended to the claimant the level of settlement shifts back up to £6599 which is statistically indistinguishable form the £6627 that prevailed when the English rule alone was in force. These shifts in settlement level are empirically more modest than suggested by our theoretical analysis above, but are certainly in the predicted directions.

These results, then, suggest that the various cost-shifting rules available in British courts do not have a measurable impact on the propensity to come to a pre-trial settlement, at least as measured in these experiments. The impact on the level of pre-trial settlement is significant, however, if somewhat less in magnitude than suggested by theory. The defendant offer (payment into court) places the defendant at a negotiating advantage. This advantage is countered, however, when the claimant is also allowed to make such offers (with their potentially significant impact on the amount of legal costs paid by each of the parties).

Now, we turn to the evidence from the experiments involving professionals. The eight practitioner solicitors played two games of each of the cost-rule types. As a pair of participants (defendant and claimant) is required for each game, this gave eight games of each type. The 36 post-graduate law students each played four games of defendant payments into court and two-way offers to settle respectively, giving 72 games of each of these two types, and the 18 MBA's played three games each of the English rule alone and defendant payments into court, giving a total of 27 games of each type. The results obtained are available in Tables 4, 5 and 6.

The small number of games played by the practitioners[18] means that it is very

Table 4. Impact of varying cost rules (Practitioner solicitors)

	English rule alone	Defendant offers	Two-way offers
Settlements (%)	8 (100%)	6 (75%)	5 (63%)
Trial (%)	0 (0%)	2 (25%)	3 (27%)
No. of games	8	8	8
Average Settlement (£)	5863	5617	5540
St. Deviation	573	1030	428
Max. (£)	6600	7000	6200
Min. (£)	5000	4500	5000

[18] In spite of the generous co-operation of The Law Society of Scotland, we found it difficult to attract anything but a modest number of volunteer participants from among the large legal community of solicitors in the Edinburgh area.

Table 5. Impact of varying cost rules (MBAs)

	English rule alone	Defendant offers
Settlements (%)	18 (66.7%)	15 (55.6%)
Trial (%)	9 (33.3%)	12 (44.4%)
No. of games	27	27
Average Settlement (£)	7072	7340
St. Deviation	804	606
Max. (£)	9000	8800
Min. (£)	5900	6500

difficult to draw any conclusions from Table 4. However, it can be seen that as cost-shifting rules are added, the number of settlements actually falls. The settlement rates are 100% under the English rule alone, 75% with the introduction of defendant offers into court and 63% with the introduction of two-way offers to settle. This is in line with the interpretation of the theoretical background outlined above – the introduction of cost-shifting rules reduces the zone of possible agreement (Zopa) and thus makes settlement less likely. On the other hand, the movement in the level of pre-trial settlement is extremely modest. It falls, as predicted by theory, when defendant offers are allowed, but it fails to increase when the negotiating power is equalised with the addition of claimant offers (in the two-way offers when both parties are allowed to make offers into court). Needless to say, owing to small numbers, it is impossible to draw statistically significant conclusions form these results

The MBA students whose results are presented in Table 5 (27 games each of English rule alone and of defendant payments into court) also show a declining rate of settlement (from 66.7% to 55.6%) with the introduction of defendant payments into court. Again, in this sense, the predictions of the theory are matched. In terms of the level of settlement, however, the movement of the average level of settlement when defendant offers are allowed is exactly opposite to that which we would predict. It seems that the defendants in these experiments failed, in general, to utilise to their advantage this addition to their bargaining power. But, again, low numbers make it difficult to draw statistically robust conclusions here.

These two sets of results are in contrast to the results for the remaining professional participant types. The post-graduate law students provide a more statistically significant sample of 72 games per cost rule (the two cost rules deployed being defendant payments into court and two-way offers to settle). From Table 6, it can be seen that in this case the settlement rates are identical at 73.6% for both rules. Recall that in Table 3 the large samples of undergraduate students (114 games for English rule alone, 222 games for defendant payments into court and 108 games for two-way offers to settle) finds that the settlement rates are again broadly similar across cost-rules (72.8%, 73.9% and 71.3% respectively).

Certainly more puzzling, in the case of the post-graduate law students, is the failure of settlement level to be influenced by the move in cost-shifting rule from defendant offers only to two-way offers. This would have been predicted

Table 6. Impact of varying cost rules (Post Graduate Law students)

	Defendant offers	Two-way offers
Settlements (%)	53 (73.6%)	53 (73.6%)
Trial (%)	19 (26.4%)	19 (26.4%)
No. of games	72	72
Average Settlement (£)	6340	6381
St. Deviation	1240	916
Max. (£)	9000	7900
Min. (£)	700	2000

by theory (and confirmed in experiments involving the undergraduates) to restore some bargaining power to the claimant, thus shifting the pre-trial settlement level higher. This singularly fails to happen with the PG law students whose negotiating behaviour seems singularly unaffected by the type of cost-shifting rule in place. This is particularly surprising, given the recent immersion in the intricacies of these rules that forms part of their post-graduate studies.

Dynamics

Although the main thrust of these experiments is to focus on the impact of various cost-shifting procedural rules on both the propensity to reach pre-trial settlement and the level of that pre-trial settlement, the data collected also allow some insights into the dynamics of the bargaining process. We will focus exclusively on the behaviour of the undergraduate participants described above, as these were the most statistically robust observations owing to the much higher numbers involved. In all of the negotiations, events were structured such that the claimant always had the initial or opening demand.

There are several distinct aspects of the so-called 'negotiation dance[19],' that merit our attention. One concerns the importance of the opening bid in anchoring the subsequent negotiation and thereby influencing its outcome. Basically, the question is do high opening demands lead to high settlements (and vice versa)? Another is whether the propensity to reach a settlement (as opposed to impasse, i.e. trial in this context) is a function of the difference between the parties at the outset. Thus, is the size of the spread between initial claimant demand and initial defendant offer related to the probability of reaching a pre-trial settlement? This consideration could affect the extent to which authorities wish to ensure full revelation of all material evidence and opinion relating to the case in hand (discovery). Related to this we may wish to consider the impact of the opening spread on the level of settlement in those cases which reach pre-trial settlement. There is also the question of the number of bids, and whether more frequent communication of bid and counter bid is likely to increase the chances of reaching a pre-trial settlement.

These various aspects of the negotiation dance are addressed in four charts

---

[19] See Raiffa (1982) for a classic discussion of the process of negotiation.

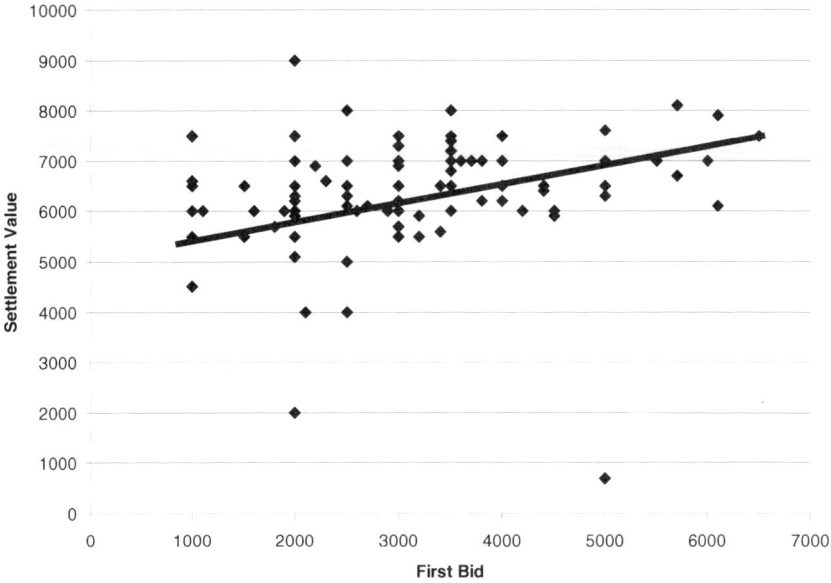

Chart 1. Settlement Value against First Bid

discussed below. In the first, Chart 1, the claimant opening demand is plotted on the x-axis. We can see that there is an empirically modest, although significant, relationship between high opening demands and subsequent high settlement values.

But this phenomenon has to be balanced against the effect that arises when the opening positions are far apart (likely to happen when the opening demand is high or the opening offer is low). As can be seen in Chart 2, which plots the percentage of cases reaching settlement on the x-axis against the size of the initial demand-offer spread on the x-axis. Here, there is a negative relationship between the size of the opening spread between the positions of the two parties and the proportion of cases reaching a pre-trial settlement. In addition, the impact of the high opening spread on the level of settlement among those cases which do reach successful pre-trial agreement is limited and apart from some initial success (whereby a very low spread is associated with a modest level of settlement) there seems to be little impact on the level of settlement whether the initial gap between the parties is large or very large. These effects are clear in Chart 3 which plots the settlement value on the y-axis against the size of the opening demand-offer spread on the x-axis.

The final dimension of the negotiation dance examined is the influence of the number of bid exchanged between the parties. Chart 4 plots the average settlement rate on the y-axis against the total number of bids on the x-axis. This shows a decrease in the probability of settlement as the number of bids increases. This is not, altogether, surprising as a large number of bids indicates a failure to reach agreement. On the other hand the more bids there are then the

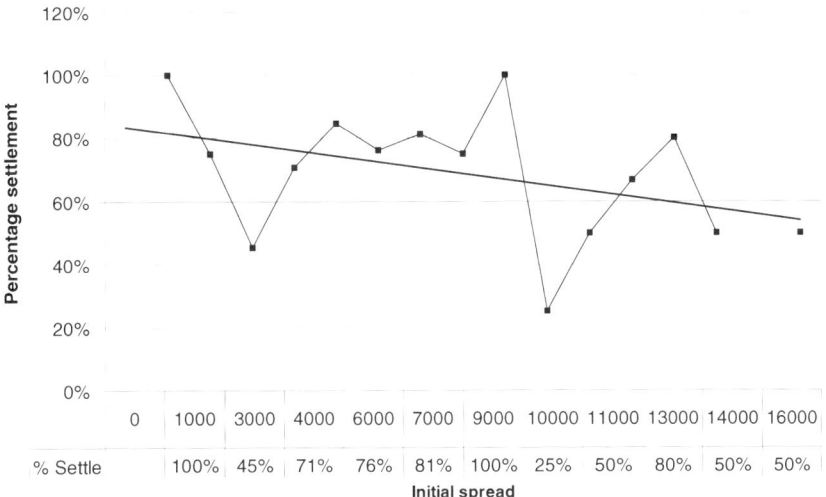

Chart 2. Percentage that Settle against Initial Spread

greater the communication and the more that the parties are able to discern each other's position and interests. One could easily envision procedural arrangements that might be designed to facilitate such increased pre-trial communication. Indeed moves to introduce mediation into pre-trial protocols can be viewed in this light. It is also worth bearing in mind that in the experiments from which these data are derived, there is a time limit on each negotiation

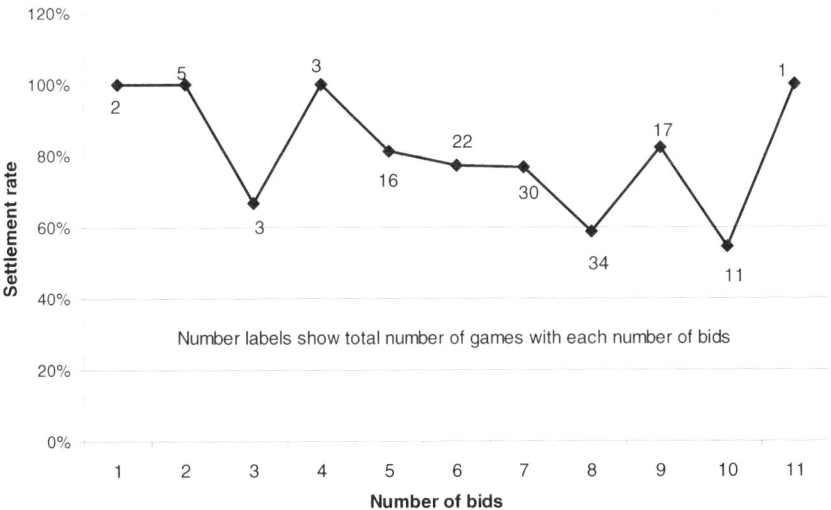

Chart 3. Percentage that Settle against Number of Bids

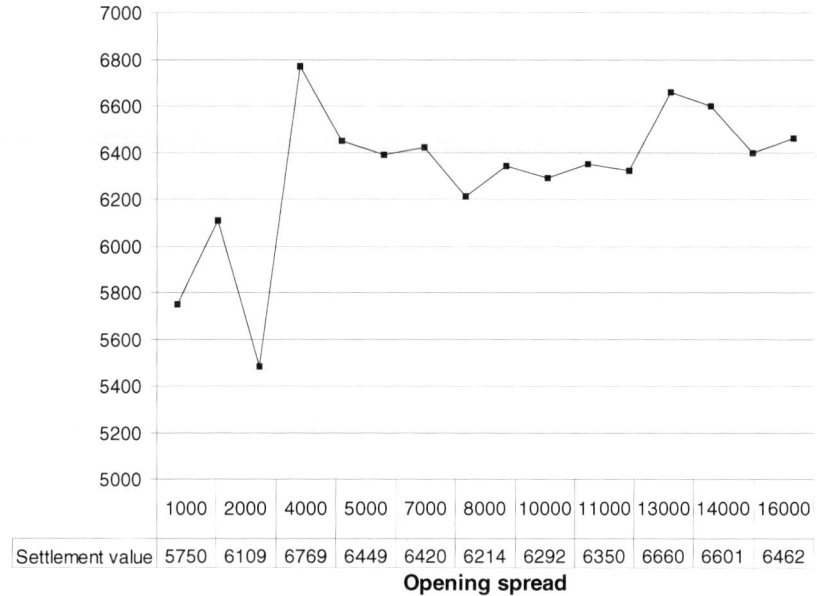

Chart 4. Settlement Value against Opening Spread

game (three minutes). While cases in the real world have a judicial timetable that leads them inexorably toward trial and the courtroom, and while modern procedural reform along the lines of Lord Woolf's case management enforces this timetable, the matter is much more in the hands of the litigating parties in the real world than in these experiments.

But putting the evidence from these four charts together, we are left with the following picture. A claimant opening high will have more chance of securing a high level of settlement. But if the spread between the parties in opening positions is large then the chances of settlement are lower. However, higher spreads seem to have very limited impact on the final level of settlement if settlement is achieved. And as the number of bids increases the chance of settlement appears to fall. The overall implications of this seems to be that if the claimant opens high and the defendant responds in a way that leaves not too large a gap between the positions of the parties, then there is a good chance that the claimant will secure a high settlement. If, on the other hand, as a consequence of the low opening offer the gap between the parties is large then there is less chance of settlement and increasing the number of bids will not help. In addition, even in those cases that do reach settlement in spite of a high opening spread the final settlement value is unlikely to be any higher.

The challenge to the claimant, therefore, seems to be to open high but not so high as to create a large gap between the parties at the outset. As in most areas of negotiation, there remains much here that is art rather than science.

Conclusion

Several key findings emerge from the results presented above. The first is that this research suggests that various procedural arrangements that affect how legal costs are divided between the parties of disputes that end up in court do not make any measurable difference on the propensity of these cases to come to a pre-trial settlement. The second is that these same arrangements do affect bargaining power, to the extent that the level of settlement agreed by the parties is significantly affected by the type of cost-shifting rule in place. Recent procedural changes introduced after the Lord Woolf inspired changes in the High Court are, therefore, likely to enhance the negotiating power and improved the outcomes for claimants but unlikely to impact on the proportion of cases reaching pre-trial settlement.

The experimental results for the level of settlements with the practitioner solicitors, as with the MBA's, are in conflict with the bulk of the findings outlined above. For the practitioners, with the movement from the English rule alone to defendant payments into court to two-way offers to settle, the value of settlements falls from £5863 to £5617 to £5540). For the MBA's the introduction of defendant payments into court increases the average settlement value from £7072 to £7340. The result for the practitioners is almost certainly a statistical discrepancy due to the small sample size, but the results for the MBA group remain a puzzle.

The results for the other two sets of subjects are in line with the theory in that the introduction of defendant payments into court reduces the value of settlements and that the further inclusion of two-way offers to settle increases the average value of settlements. With the post-graduate law students, the move from defendant offers into court to two-way offers to settle increases the average settlement value from £6340 to £6381. With the undergraduate students, the introduction of defendant payments into court reduces the average settlement value to £6476 from £6275 and the further move to two-way offers to settle increases the average settlement value to £6599. The sample size obtained with the undergraduate students allows us to treat these results as statistically significant.

In terms of policy in the area of procedural reform, these results suggest that the design of cos-shifting rules does matter in reference to the level of pre-trial settlement that is likely to emerge. The introduction of the claimant's offer as has been done with Part 36 Offers in the High Court of England and Wales, and as is yet to happen in Scotland, does seem to be justified in terms of equity. To leave only the defendant offer (payment into court, judicial offer, tender etc.) does apparently tilt the balance in favour of the defendant. In terms of equity, therefore, some procedural reform here is justified. It is not justified, however, by any empirical impact on the propensity to settle. From the experimental evidence presented above, legal disputes are no more likely to reach pre-trial settlement if there is the option of defendant offers or claimant offers to affect the cost-shifting implication of ending up at trial.

From the initial examination of the negotiation dynamics involved in these experimental sessions, it does seem that any procedural reform that would facilitate lower spreads between the parties' opening positions would lead to more pre-trial settlements. The ability to make more offers and counter-offers seems to be less important than getting the parties to have a shared perception of what the case is worth. This speaks in favour of enhanced disclosure of information by both sides, perhaps through court appointed expert witnesses and other procedural rules such as considered by Fenn, McGuire and Rickman (2000).

References

Bebchuk, L. A. (1984). "Litigation and settlement under imperfect information", *Rand Journal of Economics*, (Autumn), **15** (3): 404–415.

Chung, T. (1996). "Settlement of litigation under Rule 68: an economic analysis". *Journal of Legal Studies*, **25**: 261–286.

Cooper, E. H. (1996). "Rule 68, fee shifting, and the rule making process" in Larry Kramer (ed.) *Reforming the Civil Justice System*. New York: New York University Press.

Coursey, D. L. and Stanley, L. R. (1988). "Pretrial bargaining behavior within the shadow of the law: theory and experimental evidence", *International Review of Law and Economics*, **8** 161–179.

Cullen, W., Douglas, Lord (1995). *Review of the business of the Outer House of the Court of Session*. Edinburgh: Scottish Courts Administration.

Davies, D. D. and Holt, C. A. (1993). *Experimental Economics*. Princeton: Princeton University Press.

Friedman, D. and Sunder, S. (1994). *Experimental Methods. A primer for economists*. Cambridge: Cambridge University Press.

Gould, J. (1973). "The economics of legal conflicts", *Journal of Legal Studies*, **2**,(2): 279–300.

Walker, D. M. (1974) .*The Law of Civil Remedies in Scotland*. Edinburgh: W. Green & Son Ltd.

Walker, D. M. (1997). *The Scottish Legal System*. Edinburgh: W. Green: Sweet & Maxwell.

Hey, J. D. (1991). *Experimental Economics*. Oxford: Blackwell.

Hutchinson, A. (1985). "Canadian Report". *New Law Journal*, January, 3–4.

Kagel, J. H. and Roth, A. E. (1995). *Handbook of Experimental Economics*, Princeton, N.J. ; Chichester: Princeton University Press.

Landes, W. M. (1971). "An economic analysis of the courts", *Journal of Law and Economics*, **14**: 61–107.

Macphail, I. D. (1988). *Sheriff Court Practice*. Edinburgh: W. Green & Son Ltd.

Main, B.G. M. and Park, A. (1999). "Pre-trial Settlement: Who's for Two-way Offers?" *Scottish Law & Practice Quarterly*, January, **4** (1): 30–40.

Main, B.G. M. and Park, A. (1999). "The British and American Rules: an experimental examination of pre-trial bargaining within the shadow of the law", *Scottish Journal of Political Economy*, February, **47**, (1): 37–60.

Phillips, J, Hawkins, K. and Flemming, J. (1975). "Compensation for personal injuries", *Economic Journal*, March, **85** (337): 129–134.
Posner, R.A. (1973). "An economic approach to legal procedure and judicial administration", *Journal of Legal Studies*, **2** (2): 399–458.
Raiffa, H. (1982). *The Art and Science of Negotiation*. Boston: Harvard University Press.
Reinganum, J. F. and Wilde, L. L. (1986). "Settlement, litigation, and the allocation of litigation costs", *Rand Journal of Economics*, **17** (4): 557–566.
Rowe, T. D. Jr. and Anderson, D. A. (1996). "One-way fee shifting statutes and offer of judgement rules: an experiment". *Jurimetrics Journal*, **36** (3): 255–273.
Woolf, The Right Honourable, Lord (1996). *Access to Justice. Final Report.* London: HMSO (July).

Appendix A:

Experimental protocol.

A briefing note outlining the nature of the fictional case[20] in which they are to be a negotiating party is provided to each defendant and to each claimant.

The key parameters that are communicated in the briefing are that: the probability of a judge finding for the claimant is 0.75 if the case goes to trial; the damages awarded in the event of a pro-claimant ruling by the judge come from a uniform distribution with a minimum of £2,000 and a maximum of £10,000 – the average award is therefore £6,000; if the parties settle the dispute privately there are no costs; if, by the choice of either party or due to running out of time, the case is resolved at trial by a judge then total trial costs of £6,000 must be paid by one or other of the parties; in general the English rule of loser-pays applies in determining liability for these trial costs, but with 'defendant payments into court', whereby a good faith offer to settle by the defendant that is rejected by the claimant and subsequently turns out to be at least as generous as the award made by the judge, then that the claimant will be liable for the £6,000 costs, even though the claimant is ruled the 'winner'; in some runs the claimant is also able to make good faith offers known as 'claimant offers to settle', and if the defendant rejects such an offer to settle and the judge subsequently awards damages at least as generous as this amount then the damages owed to the claimant by the defendant are uplifted by a penal 50%.

The time allowed in each negotiating run is three minutes, during which time parties are free to exchange bid and counter bid through their respective computer terminals by means of custom-written computer software; the software records all bids and also allows parties, in runs when this is available, to designate bids as 'payments into court' (for defendants) or 'offers to settle' (for claimants); the only cost to either side from utilising these special offer devices

---
[20] This documentation is available can be found on the World Wide Web at http://www.ed.ac.uk/~mainbg/

when they are available is that once made no subsequent bid can be less generous; participants are informed by the software of the level of the current bid and whether it has any special status ('defendant payment into court' etc.); the software also provides each participant with a running history of the sequence of offer and counter-offer in the current negotiating dyad; the procedure allows participants to negotiate in anonymous pairs, and pairings are randomised between each run; all runs last three minutes; a clock, visible on each computer screen, counts down the time remaining.

In each session participants are welcomed, allowed to read the introductory literature, and given a brief introductory review of the experiment. Three test runs are then conducted to provide participants with experience in handling the computer software and to give them a sense of experimental conditions.

Certain props are utilised to convey the experimental parameters to the participants in an intuitive way. First, a roulette wheel is used to decide on the liability. After spinning the wheel, if the ball ends up between 10 and 36 then is it taken to mean that the claimant's case is valid (probability 0.75), while a number between 1 and 9 indicates that the case is rejected (in which case under the claimant is always liable for trial costs). Second, in those runs where the claimant has a valid case, the level of damages is decided by use of a bingo or tombola cage. A ball representing every number (in 100s) between £2,000 and £10,000 is placed in the cage and, after spinning the cage, the one drawn at random is taken as the level of damages. The ball is then replaced in the cage.

Each type of participant starts out each run with an endowment that ensures that they always have enough money to pay the other party (or the court). In the case of the claimants, this is £6,000 (as having the case thrown out and being liable for all costs, is the worst thing that can happen), and, in the case of the defendants, it is £16,000 under the English rule and defendant payments into court (as being liable for the maximum damages of £10,000 and costs of £6000 is the worst case for the defendant under these cost rules) or £21000 with two-way offers to settle (again being faced with maximum damages of £10,000, having rejected a claimant offer to settle, with its consequent uplift of 50% on damages, and for the fees of £6000 is the worst thing that can happen in this case). These amounts are 'renewed' at the beginning of every run. In the jargon of the negotiation literature, in each run there is some £22,000 or £27,000 of 'money on the table' that is available for division between the two parties. Failure to reach a private settlement reduces the pot by some £6,000 which goes in trial costs.

To provide participants with incentives to negotiate, each knows that at the end of the session one of the games that are played 'for real' is chosen at random (using the ubiquitous roulette wheel) and each player receives a cash payment reflecting their outcome on that game. These cash payments vary across participant type as detailed above.

Appendix B:

Technical papers related to this project.

1. "Pre-trial Settlement: Who's for Two-way Offers?" with Park A. (1999). *Scottish Law & Practice Quarterly*, **4** (1): 30–40.

This paper, written for a legal audience, lays out the institutional and procedural considerations in terms of current policy (as inspired by Lord Woolf's report) and presents a summation of the results from two of our experiments. These results, relevant to a UK audience, show that we may have the wrong idea about the effectiveness of cost-shifting rules in inducing early or pre-trial settlement. Two sets of experiments are discussed here: the impact of allowing payments into court as opposed to the unadorned English rule; and the effect of moving from the English Rule with offers into court towards a system where both sides can make offers to settle leave the propensity to reach out-of-court settlements unchanged.

What is observed, however, is a shift in favour of the defendant (lower settlements) owing to defendant payments into court, and an almost balancing shift back towards the claimant with the introduction of claimants offers to settle. The Rule 36 changes recently introduced into the High Court may, therefore, claim to redress the power balance between disputing parties, but the evidence here suggests that it is not likely to increase the likelihood of pre-trial settlement.

2. "The British and American Rules: an experimental examination of pre-trial bargaining within the shadow of the law", with Park A. (2000). *Scottish Journal of Political Economy*, **47** (1): 37–60.

In this paper we use data from the very first experiment conducted. This was before the software used in the other experiments was successfully implemented and relied on a paper and pen exercise, although with otherwise similar arrangement in terms of anonymity between negotiating dyads and the other basic parameters of the experiment. The object of investigation here was the difference between the American rule (each side pays own costs) and the English rule (loser pays). The theoretical analysis in the paper predicted that there should be no difference in the propensity to reach out-of-court settlement but that when settlements do take place they should be higher (more pro-claimant) under the British rule than under the American rule. This shift was a reflection of the fact that the claimant had a better than 50:50 chance of winning at trial. The implication here is that claimants with strong cases do better under the British rule. These predictions were confirmed by the experimental results.

3. "The impact of defendant offers into court on negotiation in the shadow of the law: experimental evidence", joint with Andrew Park, pp28.
(http://www.ed.ac.uk/~ejaa17/cereal//papersnf.htm)

Here, we examine the empirical impact of procedural devices that allow the defendant to make, without prejudice as to liability, a pre-trial offer to settle and to have that offer influence any subsequent award of costs if the case ends up at trial. Known variously as 'payments into court' (England and Wales), 'Lodgement in Satisfaction' (Ireland), 'Tenders' (Scotland), 'Federal Rule 68' (USA), 'California Rule 998' etc., these are common arrangements. This paper develops the existing the theory present in the (American) literature to reflect the English rule and test the impact. Such rules are found to be pro-defendant in terms of reducing any agreed pre-trial settlements, but have no empirical impact on the propensity to settle.

4. "An experiment with two-way offers into court: restoring the balance in pre-trial negotiation", joint with Andrew Park, pp23.
(http://www.ed.ac.uk/~ejaa17/cereal//papersnf.htm)

Using a somewhat more elaborate theoretical model, this paper extends the analysis introduced above to encompass the procedural rule of claimants offers to settle. Once again, no significant impact on the propensity to settle is found and, although claimants' offers induces a movement in the level of settlement in favour of the claimant, the move is empirically modest (from £6306 to £6599 in the metric of this experiment).

5. "Asymmetric information, cost-shifting rules and pre-trial settlement: some experimental results" joint with Andrew Park, pp43.
(http://www.ed.ac.uk/~ejaa17/cereal//papersnf.htm)

One key aspect of pre-trial negotiation is the possibility (likelihood) that one side knows material facts concerning the case that are unknown or less well known to the other side. The influence of such effects is the subject of analysis in some of our experiments. Here we analyse the impact of one side or the other knowing the trial judge's decision regarding damages (but not liability). When the party making the final offer has more information than the other party then the situation is one of signalling. When the other party has the information then the situation is known as screening. This papers develops a relatively complex screening model to describe pre-trial negotiation, and presents experimental evidence (under all three cost rules) to suggest that litigants enjoying an informational advantage are better able to exploit any strength in their position than theory predicts. As before, there is no impact on propensity to settle but the level of settlement is affected. This suggests that discovery may be a key procedural consideration in terms of equity, although less so in terms of settlement propensity.

6. "Screening versus signalling: An experimental comparison of the British and American rules for the allocation of legal costs" joint with Andrew Park, pp32.

Extending our analysis of the impact of who knows what in the course of pre-trial negotiation, we use the contrast between the American rule (each side pays own costs) and the British rule (loser pays 'all' costs). We vary conditions to allow the final offer to be made variously by a relatively informed party (signalling) and a relatively uninformed party (screening). In this paper the contrast between the American rule and the English rule is used in conjunction with a screening versus signalling situation. In these data the screening results are, again, consistent with theory, but in signalling the informed party is, again, able to exploit an advantageous position. From a policy point of view, these results suggest that even if there were settlement advantages to be had from modifying cost shifting rules (and our earlier results suggest there are none) it would be wise to consider other aspects of the pre-trial negotiation such as equal access to the facts through discovery if pre-trial settlement is to be encouraged.